Bridging Gaps: Higher Education, Media and Society

Edited by

Robert Caine, Hilary Wheaton, and Louis Massey

WH

**WATERHILL
PUBLISHING**

ISBN 978-0-9939938-1-7

Contents

List of Contributors

Dr. Sarah Attfield is a sessional lecturer in communications at the University of Technology, Sydney Australia. Dr. Attfield can be contacted at: Sarah.Attfield@uts.edu.au.

Dr. Robert S. E. Caine's research focuses on Humane and Environmental Education and Ethics with a strong emphasis on Animal Liberationist Ideology and Philosophy. He can be contacted at: rsecaine@waterhillpublishing.com.

Charles L. (Chuck) Carney is a doctoral candidate at Indiana University (IU) and the director of communications and media relations for the IU School of Education. He is a former journalist who has taught journalism at various universities in the U.S. Charles L. Carney can be contacted at: ccarney@indiana.edu.

Dr. Diana Direiter is an Assistant Professor of Psychology and the Co-Director of the Women's Center at Lesley University in Cambridge, MA. Dr. Direiter can be contacted at: direiter@lesley.edu.

Dr. Liz Giuffre is a lecturer in communications at the University of Technology, Sydney Australia. Dr. Giuffre can be contacted at: lizgiuffre@yahoo.com.au.

Michael Lovelock is a PhD candidate at the University of East Anglia, UK. His thesis explores the ways in which LGBT (lesbian, gay, bisexual, transgender) identities are represented in British reality television shows. He can be contacted at: m.lovelock@uea.ac.uk.

Louis Massey, PhD, is an artist and an Assistant Professor at the Royal Military College of Canada. He investigates cognition and the social impacts of media and technologies. Dr. Massey can be contacted at: massey@rmc.ca.

Stephanie Patrick is a doctoral student in Feminist and Gender Studies at the University of Ottawa. She can be contacted at: spatr045@uottawa.ca.

Stephanie Sadownik is an Ontario Certified Teacher and a first year PhD student at the University of Toronto in the department of Curriculum Studies and Teacher Development. She can be contacted at: stephanie.sadownik@mail.utoronto.ca.

Gilly Smith is a senior lecturer at the University of Brighton. She researches the politics of celebrity food culture and the impact of media food narratives on food consumption and food security. Gilly Smith can be contacted at: gs103@brighton.ac.uk.

Laurie Trotta Valenti, PhD, works to raise awareness about social issues in the media through research, writing and education. Dr. Trotta Valenti can be contacted at: latrot@yahoo.com.

F. Miguel Valenti is a university professor and film producer interested in ethics in entertainment, currently director of the Quinnipiac University in Los Angeles campus. Miguel can be reached at f.valenti@quinnipiac.edu.

Dr. Hilary Wheaton is an Honorary Research Fellow at the University of Exeter in the College of Social Sciences and International Studies. She is also a member of the Editorial and Advisory Board for the Centre for Media and Celebrity Studies. Dr. Wheaton can be contacted at: hilary.wheaton@gmail.com.

Dr. John Yu Zhang is a faculty member at the China program of the New York Institute of Technology. Dr. Zhang can be contacted at: yzhang54@nyit.edu.

How Higher Education, Media, and Society Intersect: An Introduction to *Bridging Gaps*

Robert Caine, Hilary Wheaton and Louis Massey

What is Bridging Gaps?

Our goal with this edited volume is to 'bridge gaps' — as the title states — among three broad topics: higher education, media and society. Bridging gaps is about looking at social and cultural themes from a multidisciplinary and practice-based perspective, hence breaking away from knowledge and methodological silos that exist between disciplines. Bridging gaps also invites academic researchers to reach out to the public and address real world issues. To reach out, higher education professionals need to embrace popular media as an opportunity to participate in public debates and influence public opinion. Similarly, instead of narrowing our focus to academic publications, academics should use their voice and expertise to reach a wider audience by utilising opportunities to write opinion editorials for newspapers and magazines. A good example of this approach is the popular website theconversation.com which operates as an independent media outlet, offering in-depth analysis, research and news to the public from the academic and research community. As such, bridging gaps is constructing bridges between topics, between people, between approaches, and between academia and the public.

Originating from the international conference *Bridging Gaps - Higher Education, Media and Society,* held at Ryerson University (Toronto, Canada) in May 2015, this edited volume explores the many intersections and interactions among the three themes of education, media, and society. Given the nature of an edited book comprised of conference papers, each one with its individual and separate take, it is not possible to paint a comprehensive and completely coherent picture of the complex landscape resulting from the 'tectonic' meeting of education, media and social change. Each author has, however, been able to position a metaphorical stake in the ground that allows readers to draw of rough map delineating some of the important issues and interesting solutions. We provide further connections within this introduction.

Why three themes such as higher education, media and society? The reason is simple: higher education and media are key to maintaining and improving society. This is our starting point that we posit as a base assumption, from which we explore the challenges and complexities they face. The three themes also offer a natural overlap that we feel needs to be further 'collided' and 'shaken up' to see what 'falls off.' Our intention is to draw new connections, hence bridging gaps among the topics and among the various stakeholders interested in how these topics intersect. As such, this book will be of interest to media professionals, scholars, students, activists, and anyone interested in how media and education impact social transformation.

Exploring Relations and Synergies

Higher education, media and society form a highly dynamic set of topics, indeed a manifold with multiple interactions involving both traditional and new media technologies and leading, we hope, to social transformations that move the world forward, and toward more awareness, well-being, and equity. However, in the meantime, there appears to be worrisome upheavals such as the so-called crisis in academia and higher education, increasing social inequities boiling under the cover of neo-liberal market driven ideologies, and skilfully exploited media and mindless entertainment to preserve the existing power structure. Yet, at the same time, we can observe wonderful examples of innovative social evolutions enabled, among others, by new media technologies and a new sense of awareness and connection that arise from questioning the established order. The paper by Zhang in this volume provides an interesting case study of such social progress. It shows how Weibo, a Chinese social media platform, empowers the population and creates new opportunities of interactions with political powers. The author raises an interesting question: is this online interaction between the masses and the political elite, known to be unresponsive to human rights, giving rise to a new form of direct democracy?

In higher education, media studies bring critical awareness of representations and reproductions of popular personas, artefacts, processes, and practices in social, economic, and political contexts. Lovelock delves into the very essence of popular persona in his article whereby he examines celebrity athlete Tom Daley's coming out as an openly gay athlete. Celebrities carry great influence with respect to their public; the discussion that ensues over heteronormativity and whether celebrities possess a social responsibility for disclosing the nuances of their personal lives remains open for debate; some may assert that celebrities, such as Daley, have a social responsibility to bring critical awareness of 'oppressed others' into the forefront of social consciousness. From the perspective of cultural studies, critical discourse analysis of media productions enables scholars to go beyond observing aesthetic aspects and to understand social underpinnings of cultural productions. For example, Smith's paper on Nigella Lawson explores the careful construction of persona for the purposes of celebrity and commodification. Importantly though, Smith also illustrates how the public response to this construction, and the acting of it, can create an authenticity that surpasses the requirements of the screen. In a similar fashion, journalism can use investigation to educate and inform the public on the limits and potential of social systems. Journalistic facts can then become credible sources for academic research and effective solutions to critical issues in society. The issue of 'rape culture' is a powerful example, not only of journalism as credible sources for academic research, but also social commentary as a response. Direiter's paper provides an exploration of 'rape culture' in the media and our social responses as a suitable means by which to bring the discussion into the classroom and consequently connect with students. A related matter is the ethical role of media producers. Trotta Valenti and Valenti address the contentious issue of violence in film making whereby a highly controversial debate unfolds with regards to the responsibilities of film makers when producing violent-laden media products. Should film students be encouraged to give critical consideration to the element of violence in their productions? And, furthermore, do such portrayals of violence (in film) influence and/or stimulate reactionary outcomes in the real world, thus effecting and motivating social behaviour?

Furthermore, tabloid journalism uses narrative devices of gossip, rumour and scandals to commodify meritocratic fame while many news media have abandoned facts and intelligent analysis in favour of spectacular outrage and incivility; both situations act as testaments to the lack of informed opinions. In this respect, Patrick's paper in this volume draws particular attention to the distinction between news media as PR versus news media as journalism, and investigates how celebrity journalism functions within our society. Researchers in both academic and non-academic career paths possess useful knowledge and authority on many important social issues but may lack accessibility and visibility due to their more theoretical and intellectual views that are generally confined to academic gatherings and journals. However, their expertise could greatly benefit journalism and the development of progressive media, and provide impetus for social transformation. The inclusion of scholarly commentaries and advocacy in media is imperative to the development of a knowledge-based economy and social innovation based on critical thinking and ethical action. Carney's paper *Seizing the microphone* illustrates the unfortunate situation that journalists, under pressure from financially strapped media outlets and lacking tools for critical analysis, may succumb to the apparent open-access granted by agenda-driven think tanks and consequently, fail to properly report all sides of a story. Carney's paper is particularly relevant to this volume because it demonstrates how the debate about higher education in the U.S. has been distorted by politicians who exploit media, turning an important debate into a one-sided spectacle with potentially disastrous social side-effects.

We also often read about the crisis in academia due to an emphasis of higher education institutions on efficiency, commercial support, and market orientation (among many works on this topic: Whelan, Walker and Moore, 2013). As well, while graduate enrolment has quadrupled in the last decade, most aspiring PhD graduates struggle to find tenure or tenure-track jobs. Universities are increasingly hiring sessional teachers, thus limiting research and the dissemination of much needed critical perspectives by a new generation of scholars and practitioners. A related issue is the so-called higher-education crisis. Many have started to question and raise alarms about the direction higher education is taking. One of the issues is that our conception of higher education is being transformed from a public good to a private privilege, and from a social investment into business cost. The effects on society of this shift in conception are multiple, wide ranging, and potentially dangerous. Higher education is becoming increasingly expensive due to lack of public funding and competition among institutions who try to attract students with 'superficial' but expensive considerations like fancy residences and sports facilities. Carney questions the value of investment in higher education through his essay *When the news reports on higher education accountability, what does the public read and hear*? Concretely, does the money, time and efforts exerted by students pursuing a higher degree coincide with the benefits and long-term rewards in terms of securing employment and achieving career success? Carney addresses the fast rising costs of higher education and the debt acquired by students with the hopes of realising lifetime rewards for such a monumental investment. In addition to affordability, issues of 'quality of education,' 'whether students are actually learning,' 'purpose for individuals attending programs,' 'rates of completion of programs,' and 'trends in higher education' all comprise the ongoing discussion and discourse pertaining to perceived versus real value of earning a degree. One may wonder whether high student debt (now totalling 1 trillion$ in the US) further shifts higher education away from its goal of educating citizens by producing critical thinkers who are socially and politically engaged. Instead, is our education system moulding young adults into job focused consumers who work to pay off their debts while trying to emulate the materialistic life intensely reiterated by media, which has further spending and debt generation effects? Hence, due to our desire to be educated, are we increasingly becoming prisoners of an economic system that often forces us to give up our true dreams?

Another major issue with higher education is that since universities are under pressure to produce employable consumers, there is a shift away from the often perceived 'non-essential' or 'useless' degrees delivered within the Humanities, and instead towards the science/technology and business degrees. Yet one must ask whether 'less Humanities' could result in a loss of deeper knowledge about who we are and what we do as a society? Without the Humanities we may lose our writers, our critics, our voices of reason that stand against the commodification of our society as a whole. The papers in this edited collection are examples of the importance of Humanities degrees for understanding the role of media, interpreting and utilising it for greater academic growth, and critically assessing current practices in journalism.

This is just a brief and partial overview of the issues associated with higher education, including academia, and media, and how the social fabric is being affected, effectively, one might say, approaching a point of rupture but also offering formidable opportunities to reach out and change.

Launching Forward

We would not dare to claim that this book leaves no gap to be bridged. However, we started to create linkages, identified some of the overlaps and synergies, and hinted to the incredible diversity of possibilities that exist in the problem-solution space of higher education and media as they relate to social transformation. It is important to note that higher education and media need to be questioned and not merely taken in their existing form as ultimate truths. For example, contemplative approaches (Miller, 1994) and Tagore's 'learn in and from nature' philosophy (O'Connell, 2002) could be integrated in higher education to make it more holistic and connecting. Another powerful tool to be seriously considered in the classroom is 'laughter.' Attfield and Guiffre explore the idea of looking at the usual dry curricular content using a less formal approach by integrating humorous teaching methods such as the language of the teacher as well as comedic learning materials. In their article, Attfield and Guiffre remind us that comedy is a legitimate form of communication; as such, comedic approaches can be strategically implemented so as to preserve the dignity and seriousness of the curricula while allowing students a greater level of enjoyment throughout the learning process; some even say that integrating comedic strategies enhances and strengthens learning outcomes.

Education-enabled social transformation, as Mazirow (1981) puts it, happens by "making problematic our taken-for-granted social roles and expectations" (p. 124). To achieve that aim, critical thinking and media literacy – understanding and questioning the influence media have – should be high priorities in education. Furthermore and consequently, social progress should not be seen only as traditional progressive-conservative tension or strictly in its usual drive towards Western style democratization and legal rights, but as truly deep transformation in our worldview.

One may thus choose to take issues associated with higher education, academia, and media as opportunities to re-think the way we do things and start building anew. There are indeed many interesting ways in which academia and higher education could reinvent the world, starting with themselves. Academics can reach out, as we have previously alluded to, with popular media, but this may not be enough. Autoethnography (Spry, 2001) and performativity (Nandy, 2015) could take academic research beyond the limitations of linear writing and revolutionize how research is communicated, going from dry and distant to touching and inspiring. Another example is Sameshima & Leggo (2010) who wrote a paper that consists of a series of letters and poems on love and learning. This raises an interesting question: can we, in academia, transform ourselves and others by using the powerful tools of art and love?

Finally, media offer great opportunities for social evolution if we decide to fully harness their transformative power, instead of falling for market-driven mindless entertainment, and accepting them as instruments of mass manipulation (Chomsky, 2013). New media, enabled by the Internet, have a key role to play but are also subject to the same risks as traditional media and could become mostly industrial tools of sales and conformity. Yet, they also have the power to connect and emancipate. One can only guess what kind of social transformations could be born from yet to come media technologies, applications, and developments if we collectively choose to pursue a path of betterment. It is a choice we have to make and actions we have to take. Sadownik's article touches one aspect of this issue with existing technologies that are not always easily integrated in our practices. She suggests that educators need to integrate social media throughout the curricula as teaching/learning tools for encouraging collaboration and the building of a stronger and more cohesive learning community; concretely, social media is a reality of today's students and rather than shying away from this technology, teachers may find it both productive and practical to include this emerging arena that contributes students' own perspectives, beliefs, and new ways of knowing.

These are but a few ideas for further gap bridging to propel the world forward with media and education. This edited volume is hence a starting point that can serve as a platform for researchers, students, journalists, and other stakeholders in personal and social transformation to launch into further explorations of the sometimes worrisome but otherwise exciting prospects opening ahead of us.

I hope you too, dear reader, will join us in bridging these gaps and thus creating strong foundations for future social transformation.

Acknowledgments

The editors wish to thank the Centre for Media and Celebrity Studies (CMCS) and the Centre for Ecological, Social, and Informatics Cognitive Research (ESI.CORE) who sponsored the conference on which this book is based.

References

Chomsky, N. (2013). *Necessary Illusions: Thought Control in Democratic Societies*. Toronto: House of Anansi Press.

Mazirow, J (1981). A Critical Theory of Adult Learning and Education. *Adult Education*, 32 (1), p. 3-24.

Miller, J. P. (1994). *The contemplative Practitioner*. Toronto: Ontario Institute for Studies in Education.

Nandy, S. (2015, March). Selfies in Celebrity Activism: Persona in Celebrity Photography and Social Justice. Paper presented at the European FEDER Conference Public and Private in Mobile Communications. Covilhã, Portugal.

O'Connell, K. M. (2002). *Robindranath Tagore: The Poet as Educator*. Kolkata: Vista-Bharati.

Sameshima, P. & Leggo, C. (2010). The Poet's Corpus in Love Passionate Pedagogy. *Journal of Curriculum Theorizing*, 26(1), p. 65-81.

Spry, T. (2001). Performing Autoethnography: An Embodied Methodological Praxis. *Qualitative Inquiry*, 7 (6), p. 706-732.

Whelan, A., Walker, R. & Moore, C. (2013). *Zombies in the academy: Living death in higher education*. Bristol, UK & Chicago, IL: Intellect.

Media Literacy for Media Makers: Teaching Onscreen Violence in the University Film Classroom

Laurie Trotta Valenti and F. Miguel Valenti

Abstract. This experimental pretest-posttest design study extended the field of media literacy research to pre-professionals in the entertainment industry. It investigated effects of lecture, film screenings and focused discussions on media literacy general awareness, comprehension, critical thinking and attitudes following a unit of instruction on media violence designed specifically for university film majors. A unique new instrument, the *Film and Media Student Survey*, was developed and validated. A demographic survey was used to collect data on past media literacy education and media viewing habits, while evaluation data provided insights into the thought processes of film students as they considered issues of media literacy -- sometimes for the first time -- in their own lives, the lives of others, and in their future careers. Results showed positive changes in comprehension and filmmaker attitudes across treatment groups and significant positive differences in media awareness and critical thinking among students across treatment groups. Findings support research literature that holistic media literacy instruction, which incorporates aspects of creating as well as consuming entertainment products, can open new pathways of criticality about media issues. Moreover, some 90% of the young media makers agreed that the media violence lesson influenced their thinking and that they would consider material taught in this lesson when creating future media products. Media should be presented in context and with direction from the instructor.

Keywords: film, media literacy, media violence, film curricula, ethics.

Introduction

As national debates continue over effects of violent and stereotyped images on viewers, little consideration has been given to offering media literacy and ethics training to future *creators* of our entertainment products. Instilling a sense of ethicality into the work of young media makers and providing an understanding of the social, economic and cultural influences of media could help create a more thoughtful approach to portrayals of these issues in entertainment products. The following study explores whether media literacy can help future filmmakers examine their positions on social and health portrayals and consider how they will frame their future work.

Research has shown that even minimal exposure to media literacy instruction significantly changes student perceptions and attitudes about media (De Abreu, et al., 2013; Duran, et al., 2008; Hobbs, 2003; Hobbs, 2005; Kamerer, 2013; Mihailidis, 2008; Schmidt, 2012). It would seem logical to offer media literacy to students who aspire to be the creators of TV, film and game content. However, research is almost non-existent regarding what media literacy, if any, is offered to film students in our higher education centres. Even compiling accurate data on the number of students majoring in media production is challenging. This is partly because there are myriad paths to myriad careers in entertainment. Within the nation's public and private universities, film tracks can be found under art, communications, performance, journalism and broadcast umbrellas, or embedded into digital culture, business or humanities programs as well as offered in fully-realized schools of film and television. Varied types of non-university programs also exist, including those housed in technical schools, certificate programs, summer institutes and film boot camps.

Just as there is a scarcity of research available regarding this niche groups' media literacy instruction, little is known about their attitudes and beliefs about media's role in our society, the artist's role, or what contribution individuals hope to make in their careers. Although entertainment products in their many forms hold powerful influences over children and in society as a whole, we know little about the attitudes and beliefs of those who are creating these images and sending them into our homes every day.

This paper highlights new research conducted at Arizona State University examining methods for teaching issues surrounding onscreen violence to future filmmakers, as well as exploring media literacy attitudes among these film students.

The Study

Arizona State University's film majors are housed within the School of Film, Dance and Theatre. Founded in 2005 by Professor F. Miguel Valenti and based on the concepts set forth in his textbook *More Than a Movie* (Valenti, 2000), ASU's filmmaking programs integrate media literacy and social responsibility into the curriculum for all students, thus creating the first filmmaking programs in the nation to embrace media literacy on such a level. According to the ASU film production program website, students in the Film and Media Production concentration are trained to, "thoughtfully consider not only *how* to look through a lens, but *why* they should... through a unique emphasis on ethical decision making in both content creation and business practice... Issues such as ethnicity and race identity, sex and violence are examined as tools for filmmakers to use with an understanding of audience effects and the greater responsibility of artists in society." (ASU School of Film, Dance and Theatre, BA in Film, 2014 website).

For many years, Professor Valenti informally polled film students in his film classes on their opinions of media literacy and ethics (Valenti, 2005-2014). He surveyed them at the beginning of the semester and again at the end of the term with the question: Do you think ethics in the media is a topic worth discussing, or is this a waste of your time? He reports that more than 90% of students who had never thought about media literacy before or who had heard about it and thought it was not 'worth their time' revised their opinions by the end of the semester, with many attesting that the material should be required for all film students. Until now, no formal study of media literacy-infused film courses had been conducted.

Inherent in this process was creation of a valid instrument for measuring media literacy awareness of film students before and after instruction. Very few surveys exist to measure media literacy on the university level, and none were found to measure film students specifically. The *Film and Media Student Survey* was thus designed uniquely to measure changes in knowledge and attitudes about *creation* of entertainment as well as about consuming it[1]. A demographic survey collected data on past media literacy education and viewing habits of this niche group, and lesson evaluation data provided insights into the thought processes of film students as they considered issues of media literacy -- sometimes for the first time -- in their own lives, in the lives of others, and in their future careers.

Of the sample of 77 students who participated in the study, more than 93% declared themselves film majors and 87% reported interest in pursuing careers as writers, directors, producers, actors, cinematographers, editors, marketers, game designers, studio executives, lighting and set designers, crew or ancillary fields.

The pretest-posttest experiment explored four areas of media literacy knowledge acquisition: general awareness, comprehension, critical thinking and attitudinal effects of instruction. The research sought to determine if learning was more effective by screening violent film clips and/or engaging in focused discussion following a media literacy lesson on onscreen violence as well as gauging any attitudinal shifts. All students received the lecture and were then divided into four treatment groups. Group A took the posttest immediately following the lecture, Group B participated in a discussion prior

---

[1] Existing surveys created by Duran, et al (2008) and Scharrer (2006) were adapted to create the *Film and Media Student Survey*.

to posttest; Group C viewed violent film clips highlighting the lecture prior to posttest, and Group D had both discussion and clips.

Implications for larger curriculum and policy changes for the education of future filmmakers were key to the overarching question: Could consideration of media literacy issues, social responsibility and the artists' role in society add a dimension of understanding to young media makers' perspectives on their future craft? As stated above, empirical evidence and informal surveys suggest a correlation between students' understanding of these concepts and their intention to use them in future work.

Materials and Method

Media Literacy Lesson. The media literacy lecture in this study, which all of the participants received, is an exploration into the techniques used by filmmakers when creating violent depictions and some of the ethical choices therein. The lesson was created specifically for future media makers. Thus, the lecture includes information regarding media effects, but it presents this information from the point of view of the filmmaker, as well as the sometimes-ethical choices artists make as they choose how to frame, edit, direct or write a scene. The instructor explored the media maker's tools for creating experiences on film. He discussed camera angles and editing choices, responsible vs. gratuitous violence portrayals, and the media violence high risk factors as presented in the *National Television Violence Study* (1998). These factors include choice of perpetrator and victim, presence of consequences, rewards and punishments, the presence of weapons, reason for the violence, realism, humour, and prolonged exposure. Risk factors are presented as tools that are available to film creators, tools that can be used to manipulate audiences at the choice of the artist. Portrayals were presented through the lens of the war film genre. The professor illustrated these concepts verbally for all participants in this study. The lecture lasted approximately 40 minutes and had no visual component, neither PowerPoint nor video clips.

Violent Film Clips. One half of the students viewed screened excerpts from three films: George C. Scott's opening speech in *Patton* (20th Century Fox, 1970; 3 minutes); the Normandy landing scene in Steven Spielberg's epic WWII saga, *Saving Private Ryan* (DreamWorks, 1998; 30 minutes) and a scene from *Commando* (20th Century Fox, 1985; 25 minutes) starring the iconic Arnold Schwarzenegger as a Black Ops Commando waging vigilante justice on South American drug lords. These clips were selected as being illustrative of several of the *NTVS* violence risk factors, also described as hot buttons. The *Patton* scene is designed to make viewers feel the glory and honour of war (justification); the *Saving Private Ryan* shows in realistic fashion the horrors of war, while the *Commando* clip utilizes the manipulative effects of filmmaking to allow viewers to laugh at violence and thus diminish real life effects. Two of these films received an MPAA–R rating while *Patton* received a PG-13 from the MPAA.

Focused Discussions. Half of the students participated in a focused discussion following their treatment. Six discussion questions were designed by the instructor and researcher to help students develop their comprehension of the instruction and critical thinking skills as they integrated what they learned with their personal beliefs and attitudes about media's role in society and their own aspiring contributions to filmed media violence in terms of social responsibility and ethics. Both focused discussion groups were led by Professor Valenti, thereby eliminating concerns over validity introduced by instructor differences. Both focused discussions were observed by the researcher, who developed written notes and observations. Discussion groups were designed to last 20 minutes. The focused discussion questions are provided below.

Focused Discussion Questions:

1. Can anyone think of a film where the violence is completely gratuitous?
2. Why do you think it is gratuitous?
3. Which hot buttons were used?
4. Can anyone think of a film where violence is portrayed responsibly? Why?
5. Which hot buttons were used?
6. If you make a violent film and a viewer copies the violence, would you feel responsible?

Results

Overall, students gained knowledge in every factor group in Paired Sample T-tests (see Table 1). Significantly higher scores after instruction were achieved in general media literacy awareness and critical thinking; higher -- although not significantly higher -- scores were revealed in comprehension and attitudes about filmmaker responsibility. ANOVA analysis revealed that none of these changes were indicated by treatment group, however. Focused discussion and films did not *lessen* understanding, but the students who participated in discussions and watched films achieved no significantly greater understanding than those who did not. This indicates that the 20-

minute opening lecture on media violence by Professor Valenti, which all students received, provided the springboard for learning and reflection.

Table 1. Paired Samples T-tests by factor group (Media Literacy Awareness, Comprehension of Lesson, Critical Thinking, Attitudes of Filmmaker Responsibility)

Paired Differences		Mean	SD	t	df	Sig.
ML	Pre-Post	.27	.49	4.84	76	.000*
CL	Pre-Post	.14	.72	1.72	76	.090
CT	Pre-Post	.33	.97	2.99	76	.004*
AF	Pre-Post	.09	.69	1.19	76	.236

* Denotes significant differences at the $p < .05$ level

Results support the literature showing positive significant differences in understanding and analysing after media literacy instruction in general student populations. Research also indicates that media literacy lessons examining media motives, effects and analysis have been shown to enable students to think critically about the how media affects viewers (De Abreu, et al., 2013; Duran, et al., 2008; Hobbs, 2003; Kamerer, 2013; Mihailidis, 2008; Schmidt, 2012). In this study, results show media literacy also helps students examine their own role in the creation process.

Filmmaker's Evaluation of Media Literacy Lesson

The survey findings provide a rare exploration into the thinking of a group of young media makers. As there is little known scientific study on entertainment creators, this study provided some initial insights.

Students were asked to reflect on what they learned in the lesson and what importance media literacy might have on them personally as they build their careers in the entertainment industries. In five closed-ended and three open-ended items, student responses were overwhelmingly positive about the impact of the lesson. More than half of the students (56%) agreed that the lesson *changed their thinking* about creating and/or viewing media violence (see Table 2). These findings are in concurrence with those of current studies on general media literacy awareness (Duran, et al., 2008; Hobbs, 2005; Jones, 2011; Scharrer, 2006), which indicate that just one media literacy course can open up new avenues of thinking and levels of critical analysis.

When asked if the information from the media literacy violence lesson would be utilized in their future careers, an astounding 88.9% agreed or strongly agreed that they would use this material as they went on to create entertainment products in future careers (see Table 3). More than three-quarters of the students agreed or strongly agreed that the class helped them to think critically about what they will and will not do in creating entertainment products.

Table 2. Student responses to Evaluation Item 1

This lesson changed my thinking on media violence

Answer Options	Response Percent	Response Count
Strongly disagree	0.0%	0
Disagree	9.7%	7
Neither A nor D	34.7%	25
Agree	50.0%	36
Strongly agree	5.6%	4

Table 3. Student responses to Evaluation Item 3

When/If I work in the E/I, I will use some of the information from this lesson.

Answer Options	Response Percent	Response Count
Strongly disagree	1.4%	1
Disagree	2.8%	2
Neither A nor D	6.9%	5
Agree	54.2%	39
Strongly agree	34.7%	25

What did the students learn?   When asked how the lesson may have influenced them, 73% of the students said the class raised their awareness about media violence while 28% said the lesson would influence future career decisions. Students reported a new ability to think objectively about how they will create violent scenes in their own films, and a new understanding about how a filmmaker has the power to manipulate viewer reactions.

If these results could be replicated in film programs nationwide it could initiate a shift over the long-term across the entertainment industry. If young creators are exposed to media literacy material and understand possible effects of their work on their audiences, they could be empowered to make socially responsible decisions regarding their use of potentially harmful images throughout their entertainment careers. Further, if media artists use violence or aberrant images in their work, media literacy could provide a lens for them to understand the manipulative aspects of their products and choose their tools with full knowledge of their import on viewers as more than simple entertainment.

Future Work

Future work would engage university level teachers of film and media production to consider inclusion of media literacy education in their curricula in the hopes that these concepts will be taught to pre-professionals entering the pipeline in film programs nationwide. Any instructor using film and other media in his or her curricula might consider the research indicating that media is most effective when presented in a contextual setting with opportunity for discussion and reflection provided afterwards.

Further testing of the instrument is needed and further study in this area could confirm or reject the results found herein. The films clips used in the study were selected by the instructor to illustrate media violence risk factors. A future study using more current films or illustrating different aspects of violence might yield different results.

The media literacy lecture, which proved to be a very influential factor, could be difficult to replicate, as Professor Valenti is the author of the book on this topic and is an acclaimed speaker on media issues. Any discussion of artists rights or flashpoint issues such as violence or sexuality are best presented as social and public health issues and in an open environment where students feel free to air their beliefs and opinions with all First Amendment rights respected to the fullest extent.

This lecture and study on media violence was conducted towards the end of a semester-long inquiry into ethics in media making. Although the study examined the effects of the one violence lesson, the impact of the previous weeks' explorations into other social issues may have influenced students. Attempting to replicate the study early in the semester could further validate the effectiveness of a single media literacy lesson on students. A follow-up or a longitudinal study would illuminate any longer-term effects from the instruction.

Conclusions

This study found significant positive differences in students' general media literacy awareness and critical thinking following a lesson on media violence. Overall, students gained knowledge in every factor group after this lesson. Positive changes in scores independent of treatment groups indicate that the 20-minute opening lecture, which all students received, provided the springboard for learning and reflection.

In evaluation items, students responded positively overall about the impact of the media literacy lesson on their thinking and their expectations on how they will use the material in their future careers, as well as their abilities to think critically about media violence. Students discussed a new sense of awareness about the manipulative nature of media products following the lesson and an ability to think objectively about how they portray violent scenes in their own films.

The instrument developed for this study was created specifically for pre-professionals in the entertainment industry. The *Film and Media Student Survey* measured awareness, knowledge, critical thinking and social responsibility.

A broad, philosophical question that inspired this study was, could consideration of media literacy, social responsibility and explorations into an artist's role in society influence the long-term perspectives of future media makers? The results of this small study indicate the answer is yes. If more thoughtful portrayals of health and social issues can be presented in popular television programming, films and games, society as a whole could benefit

Acknowledgments

Thanks to ASU Professor Wilhelmina Savenye and to researchers Scharrer and Duran, et al, for their work on creating models to survey media literacy instruction effectiveness. Any work in media literacy must acknowledge Renee Hobbs for her efforts over many years; my sincere thanks to Dorothy Singer of Yale University for her work in television effects on children and her personal support of my work.

References

Arizona State University School of Film, Dance and Theatre, Bachelor in Film programs. (2014). Retrieved February 23, 2014 from: http://theatrefilm.asu.edu/degrees/undergrad/ba_film/

De Abreu, Belinha S, Mihailidis, Paul. (2013). *Media Literacy Education in Action: Theoretical & Pedagogical Perspective: Theoretical and Pedagogical*

Perspectives. Routledge. Retrieved 16 November 2014, from

Duran R.L., Yousman B., Walsh K.M., and Longshore M.A. (2008). Holistic Media
   Education: An Assessment of the Effectiveness of a College Course in Media
   Literacy. *Communication Quarterly*, 56:1, 49-68

Hobbs, R. (2003). Measuring the acquisition of media literacy skills. *Reading
   Research Quarterly*, 38(3), pp. 330-355.

Hobbs, R. (2005). The State of Media Education. *The Journal of Communication*,
   Volume 55, Issue 4 pp. 865-871.

Jones, E. K. (2011). A Problem-Based Learning Approach   to Social Responsibility
   in Race, Gender, and Media Courses. *Multicultural Education Journal*, pp. 60-64.

Kamerer, D. (2013). Media Literacy. *Communication Research Trends, 32*(1), pp. 4-
   25.

Mihailidis, P. (2008). Are we speaking the same language? Assessing the state of
   media literacy in U.S. higher education. *Studies in Media & Information Literacy
   Education*, 8(4), 1-14.

National Television Violence Study (NTVS) Executive Summary (Vol. 1). (1996).
   Studio City, CA: University of Santa Barbara and Mediascope (Organization).

Scharrer, E. (2006). "I Noticed More Violence:" The Effects of a Media Literacy
   Program on Critical Attitudes Toward Media Violence. *Journal Of Mass Media
   Ethics*, *21*(1), 69-86. doi:10.1207/s15327728jmme2101_5

Schmidt, H. (2012*)*. Media Literacy Education at the University Level. *The Journal
   of Effective Teaching*, Vol. 12, No. 1, 2012, pp. 64-77

Trotta, L. (2012). Children's Advocacy Groups: A History and Analysis, *Handbook of
   Children and the Media (2nd Edition)* Los Angeles, CA; Sage Press, pp. 697-715.

University Film and Video Association. (2013). About the University Film and Video
   Association. Retrieved Sept. 17, 2013, from http://www.ufva.org/about.

Valenti, F. M. (2000). *More Than a Movie: Ethics in Entertainment*. Boulder, CO:
   Westview Press.

Valenti, F.M. (2005-2013). Empirical data from informal surveys of students in FMP
   250 and FMP 417, ASU School of Film, Dance and Theatre.

Self-critique or Self-promotion: The Vanishing Gap in Celebrity Public Relations Journalism

Stephanie Patrick

Abstract. The news is a critical site upon which public/private interests converge and where public relations efforts disguise self-interest as critically informed choice. Furthermore, news presents itself as 'common sense' and is thus key in developing and circulating normalising discourses throughout society. However, under the revenue-generating pressures of capitalism, journalists increasingly have to appeal to a broader audience base and public discourses start to fall to a 'lowest common denominator' threshold wherein the numbers of people they appeal to begin to shape what is being communicated. This trend, I argue, is a key factor in the increasing pervasiveness of celebrity culture, as well as the increasing self-reflexive vitriol in celebrity news reporting. This paper will critically engage with the double PR function of celebrity news – to both promote and persecute celebrity culture – and examine how celebrity news reporters' self-critique disguises the self-interest inherent in all news media reporting: that is, to preserve the institutional power of the media itself.

Keywords: Celebrity; journalism, public sphere, public relations, Habermas.

Introduction

Celebrity culture today, with its emphasis on the commodification of public figures themselves, exemplifies Habermas' (1989) transformation of the public sphere into "a medium of advertising," in which public discourses increasingly serve private capital interests (p. 189). The ideal Habermasian public sphere was a necessary forum in democratic society where citizens could gather, debate and form public opinion (Habermas, 1989; see also Fraser, 1990; West, 2005). The rise of mass media has shifted this public debate into the realm of news reporting (Castells, 2008; DeLuca & Peeples, 2002), yet the increased pressures to conform to capitalist logic hinder the news' ability to perform their ideal public duty (Beers, 2006; Hatchen, 2004).

This contentious trend is embodied in the increased focus on celebrities and entertainment as news (Bishop, 2004; Couldry, 2008; Delli Carpini & Williams, 2001). In 2007 MSNBC news anchor Mika Brzezinski famously refused to report on Paris Hilton and, after much back-and-forth with her producers, eventually shred the piece on live television (Harris, 2007). The subsequent popularity of the video – it went 'viral' with over one million views – hints that both journalists and their audience share a sense of frustration with the current state of the field. Other, more recent instances, such as the #askhermore campaign[1] as well as the growing instances of celebrities refusing reporters' shallow (and often gendered) questions (Cate Blanchett and Scarlett Johansson[2] are recent examples), show that this frustration is shared by not only journalists and audiences, but also celebrities themselves.

How, then, can the news media fulfil its ideal, public duty when the newsmakers themselves are so heavily implicated in the construction of this cultural landscape? The news media are both public and private - they hold institutional power but are simultaneously supposed to hold institutional powers accountable. This paper will critically engage with the double PR function of celebrity news reporting – to both promote and persecute celebrity culture – and examine how media self-critique is used to mask the self-interest inherent in all news reporting: that is, to preserve the institutional power that the media holds.

Vanishing Gaps

Many recent technological and social developments have shaped today's diverse news media landscape in ways that trouble public/private binaries. Pervasive Internet and mobile devices allow regular 'citizen journalists' to capture and share newsworthy events both within and beyond the bounds of the traditional media institutions (Allen, 2009; Beers, 2006; Compton, 2000; Wall, 2015). These technological developments have both democratised and – somewhat paradoxically – commoditised access to content that now straddles the line between public and private (Castells, 2008; Lewis & Usher, 2013; McIntosh White, 2012).

---

[1] The #askhermore campaign is a social-media movement demanding that journalists on the red carpet ask female stars less superficial questions, instead of merely focusing on "who they're wearing."

[2] During her recent publicity blitz to promote *Cinderella,* Blanchett made headlines when she jokingly mocked an interviewer's question about the cat that appears with her in the film. Blanchett is also known for famously rebuking a red carpet cameraman who panned up and down to get a full shot of her designer dress in 2014. Similarly, while promoting the *Avengers* franchise Johansson has, on several occasions, called out reporters for their singular focus on her diet regime and skin-tight outfits while her male co-stars entertain questions about their acting processes.

Meanwhile, the proliferation of platforms for expression has blurred the boundaries that delineate politics, entertainment and commodity. While some critics (and former journalists) lament the effects of 'infotainment' on an informed democratic politic (Hatchen, 2004), others praise the merging of the two as a more inclusive form of public discourse (West, 2005), while still others point to the flaws of a conceptual binary between entertainment and politics in the first place (Delli Carpini & Williams, 2001; DeLuca & Peeples, 2002).

At the same time, media scholars have also been looking toward celebrity culture to understand the vanishing gap between the public and private (Dyer, 2004), as well as the relationship between entertainment and politics (Bishop, 2004; Hooghe, 2002; Marshall, 1997). The rise of celebrity journalists (Brian Williams, Geraldo Rivera) as well as the proliferation of celebrities as reporters (Kelly Osbourne, Mario Lopez) reflects these vanishing distinctions (Baym, 2005; Couldry, 2008; Hatchen, 2004). Yet comparatively little work has been done to specifically conceptualise the role of celebrity news reporting in relation to Habermas' ideal democratic public sphere.

Celebrity news reporting is unique in that it often does not display the objectivity and distance that other news reporting does (Holmes, 2010; Williamson, 2010). While certainly "gossip" sites and tabloid news reporting exhibit a strong use of personal voice (Perez Hilton's hand-drawn captions over paparazzi shots; TMZ's casual newsroom conversations), "hard news" sources regularly employ this personal tone in their reports as well – if not directly, then in their use of secondary quotes from the tabloids sourced for material.

Upon the 2014 marriage of Kim Kardashian and Kanye West – popular media targets today – *National Post* reporter Rebecca Tucker sarcastically summarises West's wedding speech: "The real kicker, though? Speaking of himself and his new family — again, we're talking about the Kardashians — West reportedly said: 'At this table … the combination of powers … can make the world a better place'" (Tucker, 2014). Even the veritable CBC cannot help but get in on the Kardashian fun, running an online story about the star's recent nude cover for *Paper* magazine, intended to "#breaktheinternet": "Despite the flurry of online activity generated by Kardashian's cover, the internet appears to be working fine" (CBC news, 2014). While *Paper* magazine gets promoted, Kardashian bears the brunt of their editorial decision to feature her nude on the cover, even from other media editors who arguably are quite aware of her lack of editorial power.

This dual role of celebrity news reporting, as both public relations officer and journalist, allows for the news media to both promote celebrity culture to its audience, while critically reflecting on the process in a new kind of 'objective' way (sarcastic and self-aware jabs). It allows them to tap into public sentiment about its own declining state in order to sell more of its own (declining) product. The news media play a key role in normalising beliefs within society, while celebrity culture promotes and normalises the values of capitalism itself. It is therefore important to examine how power relations both produce, and are produced by, celebrity news media.

Celebrity News as Journalism

In developing his model of an effective public sphere in which citizens come together to critically reflect on political issues, Habermas delineated two main forms of communication in capitalist democracies (1987). The first type, strategic communication (oriented to control and manipulate) falls in line with public relations; while in the second type, journalists strive for communicative action (open and non-coercive) in pursuing public interest (Compton, 2000; Habermas, 1987; McIntosh White, 2012).

To return to the CBC example on Kardashian's nude photo shoot, the story itself served to bolster the public awareness of an otherwise obscure magazine and a trending hashtag, while the 'public interest' component included a weighing of the pros and cons of a mother posing nude, as well as a 'cheeky' self-aware reference (reassurance) to Kardashian's lack of institutional power (to, in fact, #breaktheinternet).

Celebrity news necessitates the mention (and therefore, promotion) of private capital-based interests. Celebrities are not political public figures, they represent a product – either themselves or a film, show, etcetera to which their brand is tied. Celebrity reporting is thus bound to fail as a journalistic endeavour. Yet in many ways contemporary journalism fails in this endeavour beyond the realm of celebrity culture. The increased pressures of news media to conform to market values means, not only a shift toward consolidated ownership and increased advertising (Beers, 2006; Habermas, 1989), but also a shift toward news content that obeys market logic.

Fairclough (1988) argues that pressures to attract more of the market share have shifted news producers to take a lowest common denominator approach to production (p. 132). In order to maximise their appeal, 'newsgivers' (i.e. the journalists/anchors who present the news) present themselves as peers to their audience. They develop a "relationship of solidarity" (consumer loyalty) with the audience and "can mediate newsworthy events to the audience in the latter's 'common sense' terms" (Fairclough, 1988, p. 132).

As Compton (2000) has pointed out, however, the consolidation of ownership into the hands of the elite creates a 'common sense' that reflects, not the interests or sense of the public, but the values of those elite who own the news media (see also Beers, 2006). The news media "legitimize and reproduce existing asymmetrical power relationships by putting across the voices of the powerful as if they were the voices of 'common sense'" (Fairclough, 1988, p.133).

One way to escape this trend, as Beers (2006) observes, is through independent news[3] where, increasingly, the 'newsgivers' present their own views rather than act as a mediator dispensing elite views. However, independent journalists often have similar training to those working in mainstream news and thus use similar cues and forms of presentation that imply a 'common sense' viewpoint being shared with the reader or watcher of news. This can be problematic when such common sense views overlook or purposefully distract from other power relations in society. Such concerns are exemplified well in the gendered reporting on celebrity culture that frames 'talent' and 'work' as common sense terms rather than subjective and/or historically and socially inflected ones (Holmes, 2010).

Such common sense notions vis-à-vis celebrities speak to a wider appeal of celebrity culture that crosses demographic boundaries. This broad appeal of celebrity news makes it a necessary encumbrance on news organisations operating on profit. When reporting on celebrity news the newsgiver will often step outside the journalist frame and use a personal voice reflecting their 'common sense' take on the nuisance that is celebrity culture.

Brzezinski's on-air rant is just one memorable example of this 'common sense' take in recent years. Surveys of journalists demonstrate concern that news and entertainment are no longer distinct (Hatchen, 2004, p. 86), and staff cuts in news organisations are producing an "industry that is more undermanned and unprepared to uncover stories, dig deep into emerging ones or to question information put into its hands" (Pew Research Center, 2013).

Such concerns speak to an idealised model of journalism that is separate and distinct from public relations, according to the forms outlined by Habermas (1987). If celebrity news reporting is not journalism, it should, within this binary framework, fit into the category of public relations.

---

[3] Beers' (2006) definition of independent news includes a variety of formats, all of which are "owned, operated, and structured to allow reporting and commentary that compensates for and counters the corporate media consensus" (p. 116).

Celebrity News as Public Relations

Public relations professionals are sought out in order to "buy influence and impose private understandings of reality" (McIntosh White, 2012, p. 566). Though Habermas (1989) laments the intrusion of private interests into the public sphere, he acknowledges that public relations is more complex than these binaries might at first allow: "[public relations] bestows on its object the authority of an object of public interest about which – this is the illusion to be created – the public of critically reflecting private people freely forms its opinion" (p. 194).

This illusion of critically formed opinion is key to understanding the critical reporting on celebrity culture. In many cases the celebrity is *not* presented unquestioned, as persons whose products should, by common sense standards, be bought by consumers (of both news and celebrity culture). Again, the *National Post*'s questioning of Kanye West's assertion that he and the Kardashians might be able to make the world a better place undermines the fact that his music is not only a validated form of contemporary art, but also is a lucrative product enjoyed by millions of consumers who look to news media to find out more about his latest products.

However, this critical questioning in the news is not exclusive to the realm of celebrities and, as Compton (2000) notes, the critical voice has long played an important role in contemporary North American journalism. Gitlin (1991) calls this self-aware critical news "metacoverage" and points out that the audience is "invited to be *cognoscenti* of their own bamboozlement" (p. 122, emphasis in original).

If both the audience and the journalist are knowingly bamboozled, who benefits? Certainly the celebrities benefit from the publicity of being reported on but so, too, do the elite media owners who generate profit through such reporting. Self-reflexive critique in the media, however, rarely aims its critique at the latter group (a structural critique) rather than the former (an individual critique). The critique thus remains superficial, as media producers deflect responsibility for, not only their own complicity in the system, but also their exploitation of it (see also Bishop, 2000).

Aiming a critique at celebrity culture is thus strategic rather than incidental. It absolves journalists of recognising that celebrity culture is a structural feature of media. Journalists are in the business of legitimising the media itself and thus their critiques do little besides amass 'common sense' frustration with a stable and comprehensive structure from which they benefit.

Conclusion

To return to earlier themes, the vanishing gap between public and private can actually offer an alternative, non-binary framework for re-conceptualising today's celebrity journalism – and, by extension, other forms of journalism. Many critics have pointed out the insufficiencies of Habermas' model in contemporary times when there are multiple sites of public debate, multiple kinds of publics, and increasing convergence between public/private interests (Castells, 2008; Compton, 2000; Fraser, 1990).

DeLuca and Peeples' (2002) conception of the "public screen" offers an alternative to the public sphere wherein "the most important, public discussions take place via 'screens'— television, computer, and the front page of newspapers" (p. 131). In fact, they argue that the "public screen" offers audiences a chance to "hold corporations accountable" (p. 134) in a way that journalists working for large corporations no longer can. The line between journalist and public relations officer is blurred, but so too is the line now between citizen and journalist; audience and news.

What, then, might celebrity news reporting look like in this new model? If the 'public screen' offers the opportunity for democratised access, perhaps there is room for a new kind of celebrity culture to emerge – one that does not so clearly espouse the values of private capital. The rise of new forms of 'democratised' celebrity (reality television, *Youtube* stars), has weakened the institutionalised media's role as gatekeeper. The increasing ability of those in the entertainment realm to 'talk back' to the media has transformed one-way models of communication into more multiple, transparent and accountable forums of public debate (Jon Stewart's news satire; Cate Blanchett's questioning of reporters' questions; celebrities using Twitter to speak 'directly' to their fans).

Self-critique can be a seductive way to build empathy and consent just as much as it can be a powerful force driving transformation. When legitimised members of the media indulge in such critique then, we must question whose interests are ultimately being served and what is being obscured.

References

Allen, S. (2009). Histories of citizen journalism. In S. Allen, & E. Thorsen (Eds.), *Citizen journalism: Global perspectives (volume 1)* (pp. 17-31). New York: Peter Lang Publishing, Inc.

Baym, G. (2005). *The Daily Show*: Discursive integration and the reinvention of political journalism. *Political Communication, 22*(3), 259-276.

Beers, D. (2006). The public sphere and online, independent journalism. *Canadian Journal of Education, 29*(1), 109-130.

Bishop, R. (2000). Good afternoon, good evening, and good night: *The Truman Show* as media criticism. *Journal of Communication Inquiry, 24*(1), 6-18.

Bishop, R. (2004). The accidental journalist: Shifting professional boundaries in the wake of Leonardo DiCaprio's interview with former President Clinton. *Journalism Studies, 5*(1), 31-43.

Castells, M. (2008). The new public sphere: Global civil society, communication networks, and global governance. *The Annals of the American Academy of Political and Social Science, 616*(1), 78-93.

CBC News. (2014, November 12). Kim Kardashian bares butt in naked *Paper* magazine cover - arts & entertainment - CBC news. Retrieved March 30, 2015 from http://www.cbc.ca/news/arts/kim-kardashian-bares-butt-in-naked-paper-magazine-cover-1.2832188

Compton, J. (2000). Communicative politics and public journalism. *Journalism Studies, 1*(3), 449-467.

Couldry, N. (2008). Mediatization or mediation? alternative understandings of the emergent space of digital storytelling. *New Media & Society*, 10(3), 373-391.

Delli Carpini, M. X., & Williams, B. A. (2001). Let us infotain you: Politics in the new media environment. In W. L. Bennett, & R. M. Entman (Eds.), *Mediated politics: Communication in the future of democracy* (pp. 160-181). New York & Cambridge: Cambridge University Press.

DeLuca, Michael K., & Peeples, J. (2002). From public sphere to public screen: Democracy, activism, and the "violence" of Seattle. *Critical Studies in Media Communication, 19*(2), 125-151.

Fairclough, N. (1988). Discourse representation in media discourse. *Sociolinguistics, 17*(2), 125-139.

Fraser, N. (1990). Rethinking the public sphere: A contribution to the critique of actually existing democracy. *Social Text,* (25/26), 56-80.

Gitlin, T. (1991). Bites and blips: Chunk news, savvy talk and the bifurcation of American politics. In P. Dahlgren, & C. Sparks (Eds.), *Communication and citizenship: Journalism and the public sphere* (pp. 119-136). London & New York: Routledge.

Habermas, J. (1987). *The theory of communicative action*. Boston: Beacon Press Books.

Habermas, J. (1989). *The structural transformation of the public sphere: An inquiry into a category of bourgeois society*. Cambridge, Mass.: MIT Press.

Harris, P. (2007, July 1). Why I said 'no' to Paris Hilton mania - Media - The Guardian. Retrieved March 30, 2015, from http://www.theguardian.com/media/2007/jul/01/broadcasting.tvnews

Hatchen, W. A. (2004). *The troubles of journalism: A critical look at what's right and what's wrong with the press.* Mahwah, New Jersey: Lawrence Erlbaum.

Holmes, S. (2010). Dreaming a dream: Susan Boyle and celebrity culture. *The Velvet Light Trap, 65*(1), 74-76.

Hooghe, M. (2002). Watching television and civic engagement. *The Harvard International Journal of Press/Politics, 7*(2), 84-104.

Lewis, S., & Usher, N. (2013). Open source and journalism: Toward new frameworks for imagining news innovation. *Media, Culture & Society, 35*(5), 602-619.

Marshall, P. D. (1997). *Celebrity and power: Fame in contemporary culture.* Minneapolis: University of Minnesota Press.

McIntosh White, J. (2012). The communicative action of journalists and public information officers. *Journalism Practice, 6*(4), 563-580.

Pew Research Center. (2013). Overview - the state of the news media in 2013: An annual report on American journalism. Retrieved March 30, 2015 from http://www.stateofthemedia.org/2013/overview-5/

Tucker, R. (2014, May 26). Kim Kardashian and Kanye West's wedding: Five things we know about the Florence ceremony - National Post. Retrieved March 30, 2015 from http://news.nationalpost.com/arts/celebrity/five-things-we-know-about-kim-kardashian-and-kanye-wests-florence-wedding/

Wall, M. (2015). Citizen journalism. *Digital Journalism,* 01 February 2015, 1-17.

West, E. (2005). Scolding John Q.: Articulating a normative relationship between politics and entertainment. *The Communication Review, 8*(1), 79-104.

Williamson, M. (2010). Female celebrities and the media: The gendered denigration of the 'ordinary' celebrity. *Celebrity Studies, 1*(1), 118-120.

Nigellissima: The Making of Nigella

Gilly Smith

Abstract. In this paper, food and media academic and Nigella Lawson's biographer, Gilly Smith explores how the TV cook *Nigella* was created by Lawson and her first husband, John Diamond. After his diagnosis with terminal cancer in 1997, the couple set out to maximise Lawson's earning potential with her book *How to Eat* and subsequently the Channel 4 TV series *Nigella Bites.* Smith argues that this performativity mirrored the transformation of the more introverted person Diamond had first met, and offers a fascinating paradox between *being* and *doing* glamour. Her new look was an exaggeration of the self that Diamond had encouraged and was the foundation for the glamorous on-screen image which *did* glamour with its décolletage and pinched waist dresses which would bring sexual appeal into cookery programmes for the first time. Barthes may have described the myth of *Nigella* as "ludic and aesthetic in function...the duplicity of the event is part of the spectator's pleasure" (Moriarty 1991, p.20) but this 'ludic' game with its implicit myth-making, contained an element of authenticity which Smith suggests led to the astonishing success of Nigella, the Domestic Goddess. Performativity involves a quality of interiority (Butler, 1990) and suggests that there is another self that is hidden by the player. Yet in this story of construction, Smith asks if Lawson's personal tragedy and increasingly messy narrative only contributed to the audience's engagement with *Nigella*, offering a seamless junction between the parodic domestic goddess and the dignified widow, mother and successful business woman.

Keywords: Nigella Lawson; Domestic Goddess, performativity, food, media, glamour, authenticity, construction, myth

Introduction

This paper looks at the construction of *Nigella*, the food icon, TV cook and self-styled parodic 'domestic goddess' by the people who knew her best, the journalists Nigella Lawson and her first husband, John Diamond. A couple of middle income journalists, they faced an uncertain future when Diamond was diagnosed with terminal cancer in 1997. Determined to maximise Lawson's earning potential with a book (*How to Eat,* Chatto and Windus, 1998*)* and subsequently the Channel 4 TV series *Nigella Bites (*1999), they stumbled into a heady cocktail of retro-glamour and gastro-porn which intersected with a 'masquerade of femininity' (Stephens et al, 2015) and authenticity to create a foodie phenomenon lasting over two decades.

The Making of Nigella

After the success of Lawson's food columns in *Vogue* and *The Spectator*, Diamond and her agent, Ed Victor persuaded her to write about the stories and the food that might provide the narrative of her life. The book reflected the 'real' personality of Lawson the wife, mother and food lover. Victor's advice was to be herself; "'Don't think about it", he told her "If you're too frightened or too self-conscious, it won't work'" (Smith, 2006, p. 114). The book, published by Chatto and Windus, sold 45,000 copies in hard back was heralded by the *Sunday Telegraph* as the "most valuable culinary guide published this decade".

How to Eat showed the potential for a strong, intelligent woman to subvert the role of the home cook into a domestic goddess who laughs at the irony even while she exemplifies the role. It was an example of Skegg's "performance of femininity with strength…a way of holding together sexuality and respectability." (Stephens et al, 2015, p. 9). Her brand was based on her 'self' and offered a new role model for busy, working women who love to eat and to feed their family and friends. She was a woman like 'us';

> I have a job - another job, that is, as an ordinary working journalist - and two children, one of whom was born during the writing of this book… Anything that was too hard, too fiddly, filled me with dread and panic or, even if attempted, didn't work or was unreasonably demanding, has not found its way in here. (Lawson, 1999, as cited in Smith, 2006, p. 116)

A TV show was the inevitable by-product of the book's success. Producer, Janice Gabriel explained the TV food landscape of the time;

> We'd had Delia. We'd had Ainslie and Gary Rhodes, Keith Floyd and Rick Stein. It was the time when Jamie had been on with *Naked Chef* and food had gone through the roof. Everyone wanted to know who was going to be the next Jamie. (Smith, 2006, p.122)

Lawson and Diamond knew that Nigella might offer something for the slightly older, aspirational family-oriented viewer, the food loving middle-class – people like themselves. The decision to control her image was the answer. Establishing their own production company, Lawson and Diamond took the idea to Channel 4.

> Everyone thought she would be a success. There was no doubt. It was partly her pedigree, partly the *Vogue* column, partly because the book had been very successful and was very easy to turn into TV; it was a beautifully written book and evoked a lifestyle. She seemed to be so full

of stories. (Gabriel in Smith, 2006, p.123)

A pilot was commissioned with Pacific Productions, with Diamond as Associate Producer. Director, Bruce Goodison decided to ignore the recipes and make a lifestyle show, a window into the world of Nigella.

> She'd had a lot of tragedy in her life and that gave her something that people could relate to. It was about a woman who cooks while a bloke is dying of cancer, where everyone who came into the house is a character. It was more like an Almodovar film than a cookery programme.
> (Goodison, as cited in Smith, 2006, p. 127)

Goodison's vision was enhanced by Channel 4's request for a more 'vampy' image which Diamond had already encouraged on set. She had a "fear of disappointment that the image will not correspond with your idea of yourself" (Vincent, 2004, np) which led to her dressing up

> ...in kitsch costumes, thinking to herself, hey, it's not my fault my cleavage starts under my nose, and just getting on with it. Twenty years ago, she would have disapproved of herself, but now she thinks, well, make the most of it, it won't last much longer. Yet behind the bravado, her secret self remains unseen; that's the joke. (Vincent, 2004, np.)

The performance mirrored the transformation of the more introverted person Diamond had first met, and offers a fascinating paradox between *being* and *doing* glamour. Her new look was an exaggeration of the self that Diamond had encouraged; to discard her tent-shaped clothes and reveal more of her curvaceous figure. This was the foundation for the glamorous on-screen image which *did* glamour with its décolletage and pinched waist dresses, bringing sexual appeal into cookery programmes for the first time. *Nigella,* the Domestic Goddess, had stepped into the shoes of the woman only Diamond had seen until now, and then only in the privacy of their bedroom.

Although the pilot never made it to air, Channel 4 had spotted what it wanted for *Nigella Bites*. The critics openly salivated over their copy, "She looks like the voluptuous star of a Fellini film who has come unstuck in time and found herself transplanted from Rome circa 1960 to present-day Shepherd's Bush" (Bilmes, GQ, 2001 np). Barthes would have described the making of *Nigella* by Diamond and Lawson as 'ludic and aesthetic in function...the duplicity of the event is part of the spectator's pleasure' (Moriarty 1991, p. 20). The implicit myth-making, contained an element of authenticity which may explain the astonishing success of Nigella, the Domestic Goddess. Sensing the authenticity of its origin, it was the motivation of the myth-makers, Diamond and Lawson that engaged the audience and made the myth work. It was not to be taken literally. In a comparison with Martha Stewart's Domestic Goddess 'hyperreal projection,' Magee says

> In the mythological narrative that Stewart has so carefully and obsessively constructed, the image overtakes the person creating the image and becomes more real than the reality. Nigella self-consciously prods the image, manipulating it ironically to deconstruct both food Puritanism and food pornography. (Magee, 2007, p 8)

Rather than performing glamour for the audience alone, there was a symbiotic relationship between Lawson, Diamond, their production team and audience in which everyone was a winner. The construction of Nigella as seductress created an illusion based on a joke we all shared, a "pure play of appearances that is not deceptive, but rather possesses a particular authenticity" (Constable, 2005, as cited in Thornham, 2007, p 47). Their TV company was even called Pabulum Productions, meaning 'a bit of insipid entertainment'.

Yet there was a darkness about the game. As Diamond began to lose his battle with cancer, Lawson performed a role that subverted the tragic heroine. In *Nigella Bites*, she transformed the image of the domestic kitchen, not just feeding her friends and families, but revelling in her curves and reclaiming the right to feed herself, sometimes twice in one night. "The representation of cooking in Lawson's work starts from the importance of satisfying and caring for the self rather than others and in this way offers an alternative mode of representing the pleasures of domestic femininity." (Hollows, 2003, p. 184). Cracking eggs and allowing the whites to dribble slowly through her fingers, dangling pasta over an outstretched tongue before looking to camera was not the kind of performance we might expect from a woman about to lose her husband. Bordo (1998) might say that her clear enjoyment of gastro porn, a term she used as pre-emptive strike, "would violate deeply sedimented expectations, (and) would be experienced by many as disgusting and transgressive. When women are positively depicted as sensuously voracious about food…their hunger for food is employed solely as a metaphor for their sexual appetite." (Bordo, 1998, pp. 11-35). Yet in this way, Lawson and Diamond continued to discharge the norms and conventions (Butler, 1990) of death and dying and of femininity. Through their ludic performance of glamour, playfully juggling the *being* and *doing* (West and Zimmerman, 1987) they subverted traditional gender roles, giving brand *Nigella* a sense of empowerment and authenticity.

The Revealing of Nigella

Performativity involves a quality of interiority (Butler, 1990) and suggests that there is another self that is hidden by the player. Yet in this story of construction, Lawson's personal tragedy only contributed to the audience's engagement with Nigella and offered a seamless junction between the parodic domestic goddess and the dignified widow, mother and successful business woman. The performance of this *Nigellissima*, the glamorised, exaggerated screen version of Lawson did not hide the role she played at home and which was played out in the media. Instead it served to distract both the audience and the players from the grim reality of Diamond's death. In the final weeks, Lawson was portrayed in the press as the protective mother, counselling wife and nurturing home cook at the centre of a family tragedy. Her rigid frame of scripts was limited to bread-winner and strength for the rest of the family as she spent nights at the hospital with her dying husband, coming home at dawn to get her children up for school and to film *Nigella Bites*. Lawson's daily transformation into *Nigella* was both necessity and salvation.

As a final irony, Diamond paid tribute to the success of their creation. At the funeral in 2001, Lawson's brother and editor of *The Sunday Telegraph*, Dominic Lawson read Diamond's last words to his wife to the congregation: "How proud I am of you and what you have become. The great thing about us is that we have made us who we are." (Smith, 2006, p. 165).

After Diamond's death, the Nigella myth had to be maintained even if the game was no longer ludic. *Brand Nigella* had become about hedonistic excess and nostalgia with family recipes and stories woven through each TV series and book. Her recipes were remembered from her grandmother and her mother, using the subjectivity of her own storytelling to further perform the role of domestic goddess and narrativise the experience of cooking and feeding. Nathanson suggests that "the aesthetics of nostalgia might be less a matter of simple memory than of complex projection; the invocation of a partial, idealized history merges with a dissatisfaction with the present." (Nathanson, 2009, p. 324).

But Nigella subverted this idea, telling her back story as one that was troubled and beset with tragedy. Making herself the mistress of her own story would enhance the authenticity of her brand and control the parody, especially as her marriage to multi-millionaire, Charles Saatchi, was revealed ten years later as a mere performance of glamour in a controlling and unhappy home; as Thornham writes "The femininity offered by woman-as-image cannot be occupied or lived; it can only be worn or performed" (Thornham, 2007, p. 46).

Saatchi was not present in her programmes as Diamond and the children had been in the early days of *Nigella Bites*. Her kitchen in the Shepherds Bush home she had shared with Diamond was still the TV studio kitchen, earning a location fee for her own production company. Yet this helped to maintain the original myth of the Bohemian, dishevelled cook, despite the public knowledge of her new life in far more glamorous Knightsbridge. The domain of the kitchen Nigella transformed from a place of drudgery to a place of glamorous hedonism had itself become a performance, yet the transparency of the construction became evidence of its authenticity.

Conclusion

Comolli is writing about cinema when he describes the complicity of the audience in the game of narrativity; "The spectacle is always a game, requiring the spectators' participation not as passive, alienated consumers but as players, accomplices, masters of the game even if they are also what is at stake." (Comolli, 1980, p.140). Perhaps this symbiotic relationship between viewer and performer explains how Nigella's glamour prevailed as the illusion was shattered in 2013 as details of her home life were revealed in the Grillo sisters' trial. Lawson's life with Saatchi was revealed to be a pretence of glamour, a performance of independence as her former personal assistants exposed what really went on in the Saatchi's multi-million pound home. Lawson appeared to be a Cinderella in her own kitchen pandering to a controlling master who preferred to eat out and breakfasted on burnt toast.

But as the façade fell and the distance between the iconic Nigella and her audience closed, it was magically rebuilt as Lawson swept into the courtroom to have her day. Her dignity has become an enduring image, a glamourous defiance of the downtrodden woman even as the stories of Saatchi's control emerged. The overwhelming public support shown during and after the case was evidence of the complicity of her audience in the masquerade, and within weeks of the trial, Nigella was back on TV in *The Taste* on both sides of the Atlantic, performing the glamour her audience wanted from her, enabling us to suspend our disbelief. Lawson was the 'deus ex machina' in her own narrative, the goddess who would reveal the entanglement of her own plot, the construction of her own myth and the authenticity on which it was built.

References

Bilmes, A. (2001). Say what you like about Nigella Lawson. *Q Magazine*.

Bordo, S. (1998). Hunger as Ideology. In: Scapp, R. Seitz B (ed), *Eating Culture*. 1st ed. USA: SUNYP.

Butler, J. (1990). *Gender Trouble: Feminism and the Subversion of Identity*. Routledge: London

Comolli, J. (1980). Machines of the Visible. In T. De Laurentis, *The Cinematic Apparatus* (1st ed., pp. 120-142). New York: St Martin's Press.

Hollows, J. (2003). Feeling Like a Domestic Goddess: Postfeminism and Cooking. *European Journal Of Cultural Studies*, 6 (2), 179-202.

Lawson, N. (1998). *How to Eat*. London: Chatto & Windus.

Magee R.M,. (2007). Food Puritanism and Food Pornography; The Gourmet Semiotics of Martha and Nigella. *Americana: The Journal of American Popular Culture*. 6 (2).

Moriarty, M. (1991). *Roland Barthes*. Stanford, Calif.: Stanford University Press.

Nathanson, E. (2009). As Easy as Pie. *Television New Media*. 10 (4)

Smith, G. (2006). *Nigella Lawson: A Biography*. 2nd ed. Andre Deutsch: London

Stephens, L., Cappellini, B., Smith, G. (2015). Nigellissima: A study of Glamour, Performativity and Embodiment. *Journal of Marketing Management*.

Thornham, S. (2007). *Women, Feminism and Media*. 1st ed. Edinburgh: Edinburgh University Press.

Vincent, S. (2004). *Nigella Lawson: Who'd be a Goddesss?* Retrieved 20th January from http://www.theguardian.com/lifeandstyle/2004/oct/16/foodanddrink.shopping

West, C., & Zimmerman, D. (1987). Doing Gender. *Gender & Society*, 1 (2), 125-151.

'I didn't know other people out there felt this way...': Gay Celebrities and the Construction of Role Models

Michael Lovelock

Abstract. This article considers what is at stake in the construction of openly gay and lesbian celebrities as 'role models' for young gay people, taking British Olympic diver Tom Daley as an empirical case study. I argue that Daley's narrative addresses some of the ways in which gay people are made to suffer, on an emotional and physical level, by the routine workings of heteronormativity. However, the solution to such suffering which, in his construction as a role model, Daley appears to offer - transforming one's personal relationship to the self - in fact perpetuates and the heteronormativity it appears to critique.

Keywords: gay, celebrity, emotion, coming out, role models, heteronormativity

Introduction

Openly gay and lesbian celebrities have come to circulate widely in the mainstream media of the global West. That said, whilst gay and lesbian identities appear to have attained a hitherto unprecedented level of popular cultural visibility, these representations remain relatively small in number. As in 'real life' (i.e. the non-media world), the vast majority of celebrities are constructed as unambiguously heterosexual. In this context, when celebrities *are* identified as being lesbian or gay, the ways in which these figures are represented carry significant weight in communicating, challenging, or affirming prevailing ideas about what it means to be gay in the twenty-first century.

Indeed, the media have come to stand as central sense-making resources, providing images, ideas and representations, through which people are able to understand and make sense of themselves, their identities, and the world around them (Couldry, 2012). Celebrities, in particular, have long embodied normative ideals of personhood within specific social and historical contexts (Dyer, 1987). In this way, contemporary celebrity culture, as one of the most prolific pop-cultural spaces of gay visibility, is a primary site at which public perceptions of gay and lesbian identity are produced and reproduced.

Conscious of the role that celebrities play in shaping cultural ideals of sexual normativity and difference, many gay celebrities have embraced a perceived obligation to embody a 'positive' image of gay sexuality, constructing themselves quite explicitly as *role models* for young gay and lesbian people. Kate Evans (2002) has noted that mobilizations of role model discourses in relation to gay public figures, often centralize not only the actions and deeds of the individual (what they *do*), but also, on a less tangible level, what they *are*, that is, the kinds of personal and subjective qualities which they embody (p. 50). It can therefore be argued that in their framing as role models, gay and lesbian celebrities offer a crystallization of certain normative ideals around how to think, feel and present oneself as a gay or lesbian subject in the twenty-first century.

Focus on case study

A particularly high-profile celebrity who has adopted this role model rhetoric is British Olympic diver (and multi-media brand) Tom Daley. In December 2013, Daley, who had previously been presumed heterosexual, uploaded a video onto his official YouTube channel in which he announced that he was in a relationship with another man. Later that week, Daley appeared on the popular television chat-show *The Jonathan Ross Show*, where he discussed his coming out with the host, Jonathan Ross:

> Ross: There'll be many young people, young men and women watching, who may be in that situation, in the situation you were in. What do you say to them?
>
> Tom: Just even to tell one person, if you are able to tell your story and say how you feel... No one has to be ashamed of it. To be honest, I couldn't be happier.
>
> Ross: That is inspirational, and I think that's why you've become... I mean, you already were to an extent, but you've become very much a role model. And whether you're aware of this or not, you will find that you have become a very important figure to a lot of people (extract from *The Jonathan Ross Show*, BBC1, 7 December 2013).

Integral to the role model discourse is the idea that young gays and lesbians are in *need* of role models in the first place. The very concept of a role model is contingent upon the recognition that there is something deficient or problematic in the ways that some gay people think about themselves, or live their lives, and that these problems require rectification via the visibility of suitable celebrity role models. In the exchange cited above, Tom Daley is called upon by Jonathan Ross to directly address gay youth in a state of crisis, young people in need of the apparently valuable and transformative function that openly gay celebrities are perceived to provide.

Yet, Daley himself is positioned in direct opposition to the hypothetical, crisis-ridden gays and lesbians who may require his mediated guidance and support. Throughout the interview, Daley radiates positivity: his body language is open and relaxed, he smiles and laughs, and receives numerous rounds of applause from the studio audience, who are repeatedly called upon by Ross to join him in praising Daley's 'inspirational' and 'courageous' coming out trajectory. Evoking a dichotomy between the out-and-proud, emotionally-unburdened Daley, and the hypothetical, anguished 'young men and women watching', this sequence exemplifies the highly contradictory framing of gay subjectivities within contemporary popular culture.

On the one hand, the normative image of gay life has become one of happiness, pride, and emotional contentment. Above, Daley claims that post-coming out he has 'never been happier', emblematizing the 'shiny, happy' images of gay life, which have become the new pop-cultural norm of contemporary gay visibility (Love, 2007). Yet, at the same moment that celebrities such as Tom Daley are being constructed as the personification of the unprecedented transformations in gay rights and equality in twenty-first century western democracies (on a formal, legislative level, at least), reports of the *increasing* rates of suicide and mental health problems amongst gay and lesbian youths unsettle this idealized picture. As Suzanna Walters (2014) has noted, media images of happy and empowered young gay people must compete with a starkly contrasting discursive register, in which gay youth are posited as "inherently in crisis, always on the brink of abuse or self-annihilation [...] the suicidal (or harassed or bullied or murdered) gay teen as public figure of pathos" (Pp. 254-255).

The gay celebrity role model thus addresses, and works to reconcile, each of these representational frames, offering a means of transforming the crisis-ridden, anguished or suicidal gay, into the happy and content, out-and-proud gay subject. In the above exchange, Tom Daley is constructed as a paragon of 'empowered' gay subjectivity, someone who has successfully turned shame into pride. Indeed, earlier in the interview, he stated:

> [Before I came out] whatever interview I was doing, it was always, 'Are you in a relationship?' 'Who are you dating?' 'Have you got a girlfriend?', all that kind of stuff. [Being gay] was my   dirty little secret... I felt like I had chains wrapped around me... I   felt so alone and trapped in who I was, and just telling one person made me feel like so much better... [Growing up] I felt like... there was something wrong with me, I

didn't know other people out there felt this way, I didn't know it was
something that people do. I felt so alone, like, locked away, like I
couldn't say anything, like I couldn't be who I wanted to be. From
Monday I felt like I could just be myself.

Daley describes being repeatedly addressed by interviewers as heterosexual,
and feeling isolated, confused and ashamed that his intuited desires and sense
of self did not match this assumed heterosexuality. In this statement, he
therefore appears to locate this emotional suffering as a direct result of the
mundane social practices through which *heteronormativity* is reproduced.
Heteronormativity, in this context, refers to the cultural expectation that all (or
certainly the vast majority) of people are straight. As a critical concept,
heteronormativity encompasses the myriad ways in which this default
assumption of heterosexuality - the notion that sexual desire, by and large,
flows from men to women, and women to men, is embedded into the fabric of
day-to-day life, on a range of social, cultural and political levels (Chambers,
2009). Daley points towards three quotidian examples of heteronormativity at
work in everyday life: the media's unthinking presumption that he was
heterosexual, the lack of visibility of alternative sexualities in public life, and
the cultural association of non-heterosexual identities with misery and shame,
hence his description of his same-sex desire as a 'dirty little secret'.

Daley's words point towards how far, in an era of apparent 'tolerance',
'acceptance' and integration for sexual minorities within British society, being
gay can nonetheless entail an acute awareness of being *different* from most
other people, in a profound and ontological way. Extrapolating upon such
feelings, Sara Ahmed (2004) has argued that being gay in a straight world can
feel "like a bodily injury [...] one feels out of place, awkward, unsettled," (Pp.
147-148) through the sense that one does not quite 'fit' within a world
structured upon the presumption that most people are heterosexual. At their
worst, these feeling become manifest in acts of self-harming, and even
suicide. In 2014, a survey carried out by the charity Metro found that in the
UK, 52 percent of lesbian, gay, bisexual and transgender people aged 16 to 24
had said they had self-harmed, whilst 44 percent said that they had considered
taking their own lives (Harvey, 2014).

The everyday social practices of heteronormativity are therefore brought
into focus in Daley's statement, and critiqued as the cause of a profound sense
of emotional unease for contemporary gay subjects. Moreover, Daley's
celebrity narrative appears to offer a solution for overcoming the negative
emotions of contemporary gay life, a route to assuaging the feelings of
misery, oppression and marginalization that heteronormativity can produce.
Daley narrates a kind of existential journey from shame and isolation, to
happiness and pride, drawing upon the lexicon of therapy culture to evoke the

verbal disclosure of one's gay sexuality as the route to emotional harmony and stability. Coming out is positioned as a conduit to happiness and, most importantly, *self*-acceptance. As he stated, 'if you are able to tell your story and say how you feel... No one has to be ashamed.'

Therefore, whilst Daley in many ways acknowledges that his painful experiences of growing up gay are attributable to the social and structural, day-to-day workings of heteronormativity, the solution seemingly offered for overcoming such negative experiences, is located on a purely personal, and individual level. In the framework of Daley's interview, it is the ways in which young gay people feel and think about themselves and their sexualities which requires transformation, not the social structures which cause such anguish and suffering in the first place.

Closing Remarks

As a celebrity role model, Daley himself therefore stands as an exemplar of these therapeutic and individualistic discourses of gay self-acceptance, self-love, and emotional transformation. As his brand of out-and-proud gay celebrity circulates through innumerable media domains, the heteronormative social practices which Daley appears to critique as a source of emotional turmoil, are in fact perpetuated and reinforced. The loneliness, isolation, confusion and shame which Daley discusses as characterizing his closeted gay past, are construed as symptomatic, not of the ways in which heteronormativity continues to render gay sexualities outside the social norm, but as a kind of deficient or faulty relationship to the self. The 'ideal' gay subject, epitomized in many ways by Daley himself, therefore takes it upon her/himself to overcome these feelings of marginalization, and go forth into a homophobic world which remains, fundamentally, unchanged.

References

Ahmed, S. (2004). *The Cultural Politics of Emotion*. Edinburgh: Edinburgh University Press.

Couldry, N. (2012). *Media, Society, World*. Cambridge: Polity.

Chambers, S. (2009). *The Queer Politics of Television*. London: I.B. Taurus.

Dyer, R. (1987). *Heavenly Bodies: Film Stars and Society*. Abingdon: Routledge.

Evans, K. (2002). *Negotiating the Self*. Abingdon: Routledge.

Harvey, D. (2014). 'Higher suicide risk for young gay and lesbian people'. *BBC Newsbeat*. 13 January <http://www.bbc.co.uk/newsbeat/25711600> (accessed 07 March 2015).

Love, H. (2007). 'Compulsory Happiness and Queer Existence'. *New Formations*. December.

Walters, S. (2014). *The Tolerance Trap: How God, Genes, and Good Intentions are Sabotaging Gay Equality*. London: New York University Press.

Seizing the Microphone: A Case Study of a Higher Education Institution and the Messaging Battle over Education Reform

Charles L. Carney

Abstract. Public colleges of education in the United States must answer to several constituencies. As with other public colleges in higher education, they must serve their public, offering degrees, programs, and outreach to meet the needs of their locale. But colleges of education face a further constraint: they are directly beholden to state regulation regarding what graduates must achieve to earn a state teaching license. Most states have increasingly changed these requirements in recent years. Given a changing policy environment, the communication efforts of public colleges of education have become more important. Those efforts have been made challenging because education reform proponents have utilized political spectacle and media as an instruments of their strategy. In the state of Indiana, public colleges of education have battled quite draconian regulations. What is happening in that state provides an insightful case study of communications efforts and media response. Often, journalists unquestioningly reported advocacy statements as fact, accepting them as normative judgments, requiring forceful response from colleges of education. The case reveals much about problematic and dwindling coverage of education, including a lack of applied journalism resources, a lack of reporter insight into education reform, and pressures on higher education to conform to ideologically-driven state policymaker demands.

Keywords: K-12 education, media, news, education reform

Introduction

Public colleges of education with teacher preparation programs hold a unique spot in the realm of education policy and within the movement of education reform. They are subject to the matters impacting all institutions of higher education, including regulation from the state and federal government that can affect budgets, course offerings, and facilities. But they are also bound to state and federal regulations that govern teacher licensing. In recent years, considerable change to various regulations aimed at improving teaching and learning have been proposed and passed across the U.S.

The K-12 education system in the U.S. has faced a wave of reform actions couched in neoliberal ideology, which places market values on the system of social service and enable markets by replacing public services with private services (Sleeter, 2008). These reforms have included school vouchers and privately-run but publicly-financed charter schools, intended to compete with traditional public schools and force them to earn their share of the marketplace by providing quality service. Among the largest single efforts in this vein was the 2006 passage of "No Child Left Behind," the revision of the Elementary and Secondary Education Act designed by the George W. Bush administration which promoted these policies and called for more accountability on education results (Hursh, 2007).

Prior to the 1990s, when some of these market-based reforms began being implemented more widely, policy assessment of teacher education programs focused on inputs; future teachers were to be prepared in line with established standards for the profession. In the last two decades, reform movements have demanded more evidence of impact on student performance and have sought policies that link teacher preparation programs to the test scores of K-12 students. Lacking direct evidence linking positive outcomes to traditional teacher preparation, neoliberal reform proponents have pushed for non-traditional pathways to teaching. Deregulation, or de-professionalizing the teaching profession has been a necessary part of this push. Professional standards for teaching have been dismantled or watered down to allow new teachers to enter from non-traditional areas (Cochran-Smith, Piazza, & Power, 2013).

These changes have produced significant debate between the higher education community and public policymakers as well as reform-minded advocates, turning education into a highly politicized matter (Cochran-Smith, Piazza, & Power, 2013). Leaders of colleges of education have found themselves thrust into partisan politics as some bills touted by education reformers could inflict tremendous harm on the college. These leaders must tread carefully in speaking for their interests, in a forceful, but non-partisan manner.

Such a difficult balance is made much more challenging given the nature of news media reporting on education reform. The education beat is a scarcer assignment as newspapers struggle financially and eliminate specialized roles. Reporters not well versed in education policy may misunderstand or simply not deeply question reform policies. These factors combined with a politically-driven reform movement can produce misleading reports. This paper provides a case study of a circumstance in the state of Indiana, where Indiana University School of Education leadership had to correct the record on education reform reporting in the face of quite draconian measures.

The state superintendent presents a problem to solve

In the summer of 2009, Indiana's superintendent of public instruction Tony Bennett announced a sweeping education reform proposal with drastic potential impact on colleges of education. On July 28, Bennett presented to the Indiana Professional Standards Board (IPSB) the "Rules for Educator Preparation and Accountability" (REPA). Stating that "improving education starts with a high-quality instruction" (Gammill, 2009) Bennett laid out a plan intended to address the implied lack of such instruction.

The initial REPA proposal was a massive shift in state policy. Secondary education majors at colleges of education could no longer earn a teaching license under the new regulation; only college graduates with a major in a subject would qualify to be licensed. Also, the regulation removed all national teacher license standards from state licensing. Reflecting the move toward de-professionalization, teachers could add a content teaching area by simply passing a test. Furthermore, the REPA proposal would cap the hours of education courses any teacher could take for licensure, a dramatic insertion of state authority dictating higher education curriculum.

In the name of improving teacher quality, the state's education leader proposed eliminating a pathway to licensure that included preparation on teaching methods and mandating to colleges and universities how many such classes students could take. The proposal was presented to the board and to leaders of state colleges with just a few days' notice.

Political spectacle

The theory of political spectacle outlaid by Murray Edelman (1988) posits that political elites create a script designed to sell particular points of view to the public. The elites create a problem to solve, with identified "enemies" and "leaders" while masking actual problems and obscuring unequal policy outcomes (Burnier, 1994, p. 243). Political spectacle is a drama, utilizing directors, stages, actors, and narrative plots (Kahn & Smith, 2001; Smith & Miller-Kahn, 2004). Media coverage presenting the drama is crucial.

In the case of the Indiana REPA proposal, the spectacle was set by the state's governor, Mitch Daniels, during an interview published the Friday before the IPSB meeting. Daniels noted that the IPSB would "revolutionize the colleges and schools of education much more in terms of content knowledge" (Howey, 2009, p. 1). He emphasized that future teachers would spend more time studying the content they would be teaching, stating that colleges of education would have to make major changes. "They are not going to need as many people teaching what to me is mumbo jumbo," the governor said (Howey, 2009, p. 5).

The problem: Indiana teachers did not know subject matter well enough as a direct result of education college curriculum. Neither the governor nor the state schools superintendent provided empirical evidence to back the claims and simply told causal stories. The superintendent told the board that a teacher who doesn't understand math can't teach it, an inarguable fact but one that he provided no evidence of actually occurring in a single Indiana school.

Furthermore, rather than increase concentration on a subject area, the proposal would actually reduce the amount of content coursework for future teachers. Given the general education requirements for subject-area majors, Indiana institutions with teacher education programs required more hours for teacher education majors in a content area   than in comparable content majors. The Indiana Association of Colleges of Teacher Education found in looking at 80 percent of member institutions that they required more hours for secondary education majors in math, English, and U.S. history and were no more than four hours apart in requirements for chemistry, biology, and physics. At Indiana University, a physics education major could take as much as 18 hours more in physics; a math education major could take 12 hours more in math. A B.A. in history at Indiana University requires 30 hours of history content hours, while the history education major must take between 51 and 63 hours of content (Gonzalez, 2009, Sept. 20).

News media reporting on the process

Reporting on the REPA proposal consistently reflected the exact wording of the state superintendent and governor without mentioning different viewpoints. Education reformers have often received media coverage that uncritically repeats think tanks own positive descriptions of reform (Haas, 2007). The frame of coverage is often established as education is failing and needs saving (Gerstl-Pepin, 2002; Goldstein, 2011).

Several reports in Fall 2009 presented Bennett's opinion as unattributed fact or with think tank advocacy group supporting statements. An Associated Press story noted that Bennett said the proposals would improve teacher quality by requiring teachers to focus on subject matter. The story presented as fact Bennett's assertion that college students who want to become high school math teachers could major in education and take few classes in math, (Martin, 2009). The line not attributed to Bennett justified his call for changing the status quo, though the statement itself was provably false. Stories typically reflected the pro-reform view, presenting the proposal uncritically. "Indiana schools chief wants simpler teacher licensing" (Van Wyke, 2009) and "Simpler Teacher Licensing Wanted by Indiana School Chiefs" (WXIN-TV, 2009) were two early stories, the latter confusing things by oddly pluralizing the word "chief." That story provided no counter view to

REPA. The Van Wyke story cited Indiana's low rating by the advocacy organization National Council for Teacher Quality, which has consistently promoted alternative teacher preparation programs over traditional college-based programs, though the story did not identify the group's advocacy stance.

News reports hardly wavered by early 2010 as negotiations led to bill changes, most significantly eliminating the provision that disallowed secondary education as a pathway to licensure. *The Star* ran a story headlined "Teachers may need a different major" (McFeely, 2010, Jan. 8). State department of education staff still told reporters the bill would require a non-education major for teacher licensure. On March 29, 2010, when Governor Daniels signed the revised regulations, a state department of education news release stated "a degree in education by itself for these grades will no longer qualify an applicant for an Indiana teaching license" (Indiana Office of the Governor, 2010, March 30).

The first story on *The Indianapolis Star* website repeated the incorrect statement. "The new rules, which take effect July 31, will require that those who teach the 5th to 12th grades earn their bachelor's degrees in the subjects they teach, rather than getting a degree in education" (Schneider, 2010). The author contacted the reporter soon after the story appeared online, citing that line as factually incorrect. After the reporter, a state department of education spokesperson, and the author exchanged a few emails, only the author's presentation of the exact line or regulation that noted secondary education was still valid if content hours equaled the major prompted the state education department spokesperson to relent and admit that was the case. (Schneider, M.B., personal communication, March 29, 2010). The online story was corrected and the print story the next day quoted the author.

In the end, the regulations were significantly altered. The Indiana University School of Education was the most vocal in speaking out throughout the process, submitting numerous editorials, actively contacting reporters to emphasize facts, and responding quickly to ongoing developments. The circumstance revealed much about how education reform is presented to the public and what all professional communicators should consider.

Journalism standards

In a new age of information availability, the responsibility of a professional news reporter is, as it has long been, to share information as accurately as possible, presenting as many sides to a story as possible. While the pressure to share it quickly is higher than ever, the need to process information critically is also more important than ever. "Journalists will need to take a more holistic approach to information as a natural resource that has to be managed more than acquired" (Merritt & McCombs, 2014, p. XV). As news break more by the hands of non-journalists through tools such as Twitter, journalists must sift through the information to discern what truly qualifies as news, whether the information is verifiable, and if it answers the age-old who, what, where, when, why, and how questions.

Such management is made more difficult because the journalism industry is in economic flux. Traditional news outlets have increased competition, but newspapers in particular are losing readers and revenue, forcing organizations to cut costs while simultaneously trying to compete and restructure (Hollifield, 2011). This has often meant layoffs of newspaper staff, including at *The Indianapolis Star*, where the paper recently moved out of its downtown home of 100 years for a smaller facility and—in the latest of several years of cuts—reduced staff and management by 15 percent, including the entire staff of copy editors.

Perhaps because of the changing structure of the paper itself, during the eight month timeline of this case study, as many as seven different reporters for the *Star*—the state's largest newspaper—reported on the REPA process. The signing ceremony that concluded the process was covered by a reporter who was a veteran political reporter, but one who had never covered the REPA story before and did not regularly cover education.

Goldstein (2011) notes that journalists generally lack experience in judging validity of education policies and research, and often equate studies by partisan research groups with credible peer-reviewed work. The more experienced political actors become involved in education policy, the more purveyors of such reform will attempt to take advantage of reporters lacking knowledge. Furthermore, think tanks and advocacy organizations consistently present themselves with titles that do not identify their point of view other than being for education quality, making it even harder for uninformed reporters to discern advocacy. In this case, those organizations supported the REPA changes and provided a narrative to reform proponents that was rarely questioned except by the schools of education.

Without the critical questioning of reporters and editors regarding a reform narrative, the "schools are failing" storyline prevails. In a telling move that illustrates the normative quality of the reform messaging, *The Indianapolis Star* recently created an "education watchdog" reporter. The title implies brokenness of the system and necessarily frames the coverage. That role was created after the *Star* laid off a veteran reporter who was assigned to cover K-12 education.

Reporters are competing to report news fast and first. Discerning motive behind those either advocating for an education reform proposal or speaking against it takes time—something of which reporters increasingly have less—and resources—something made challenging when economic realities force a long-established news organization to make cuts so deep it eliminates the fact-checking copy editors. Managing the information is more difficult than ever for reporters seeking accuracy.

Conclusions

The circumstances of this case study reflect expansive use of political spectacle in an attempt to push through neoliberal education reform. This is not unique, as reflected in a case where parents sought 'choice' because of what they said were falling achievement scores when the scores were actually on the rise (Miller-Kahn & Smith, 2001) and when Arizona's governor denounced new education standards for the state proclaiming more standardized testing for accountability was needed (Smith & Miller-Kahn, 2004). Recent movements to curb teachers unions in Wisconsin and Kansas did little to address classroom performance, but raised unions as a political enemy. Such tactics may be the 'new normal' in the current climate.

Stakeholders in information accuracy must be prepared to inform and re-emphasize points refuting the spectacle. Such a response is more necessary given fewer and less knowledgeable reporters covering the education beat. Education reform proponents who proclaim a failing system are carrying the day in messaging, enabled by political spectacle. The evidence presented here is only a small sample of opinion reported as fact. Given the importance of education in a democratic society, reporters covering reform should make certain that all parties speaking on all sides of proposed change are accurately portrayed in news articles. Schools of education, think tanks, reform organizations, and politicians who support or oppose reforms should be consistently identified with the groups that support them and/or their ideological homes. Organizations like the National Council for Teacher Quality should always be identified as an organization that promotes alternative pathways to teacher preparation; in the same vein, while it is more inherently obvious, schools of education should be identified as seeking to preserve their programs of preparing teachers.

Funding sources for politicians should be more thoroughly probed and presented in stories about government officials supporting reforms. Particularly given the overall nature of the neoliberal view of replacing public services with private suppliers, these sources often may have financial interests at stake in pushing through reform. The public cannot be best informed about the changes being sought without this information. Of course, the relative paucity of education reporters can make such reporting more difficult. Instead of "watchdog" education reporters, perhaps news organizations could dedicate staff to digging more thoroughly through public records in general—covering all areas of public policy—which would allow for more informed presentation of wide areas of public debate.

This case study suggests political spectacle is an established mechanism that works to define the battle over messaging in education reform for the foreseeable future. Institutions must prepare to make their case to media in the midst of it. Awareness on both sides is necessary for the public to be served.

Acknowledgments

A discussion of this case study as a matter of higher education leadership can be found in this previously-published paper: Gonzalez, G., & Carney, C. (2014) "Challenging the spectacle: A case study on education policy advocacy." *International Journal of Leadership and Change*, 2 (1), 19-27. http://digitalcommons.wku.edu/ijlc/vol2/iss1/3

References

Burnier, D.L. (1994). Constructing political reality: Language, symbols, and meaning in politics: a review essay. *Political Research Quarterly, 47*(1), 239-253.

Cochran-Smith, M., Piazza, P., & Power, C. (2013). The politics of accountability: Assessing teacher education in the United States, in *The Educational Forum 77(1)*, 6-27. Taylor & Francis Group.

Edelman, M. (1988). *Constructing the political spectacle.* Chicago, IL: University of Chicago Press.

Gammill, A. (2009, July 29). Teacher training faces overhaul. *The Indianapolis Star*. Retrieved September 15, 2013, from http://www.indystar.com/article/20090729/NEWS/907290376/Education+training +faces+overhaul

Gerstl-Pepin, C.L. (2002). Media (mis) representations of education in the 2000 presidential election. *Educational Policy, 16*(1), 37-55.

Goldstein, R.A. (2011). Imaging the frame: Media representations of teachers, their unions, NCLB, and education reform. *Educational Policy, 25*(4) 543-576.

Gonzalez, G.M. (2009, Sept. 20). Education majors already get more content in the subjects they teach. *The Herald-Times.* Retrieved March 13, 2015, from http://ww.heraldtimesonline.com//stories/2009/09/20/digitalcity.qp-6786894.sto?code=051f8a8c-cc08-11e4-afc8-13bbeea8c6e7

Haas, E. (2007). False equivalency: Think tank references on education in the news media. *Peabody Journal of Education, 82*(1) 63-102.

Howey, B. (2009, July 23). A 'revolution' begins... next week. *Howey Politics Indiana.* Retrieved March 29, 2015, from http://www.in.gov/library/files/HPR14z44.pdf.

Hursh, D. (2007). Assessing No Child Left Behind and the rise of neoliberal education policies. *American educational research journal, 44*(3), 493-518.

Indiana Office of the Governor (2010, March 30). Governor approves new teacher licensing regulations [press release]. Retrieved March 15, 2015, from http://www.in.gov/activecalendar/EventList.aspx?fromdate=1/1/2010&todate=12/31/2010&display=Month&type=public&eventidn=61983&view=EventDetails&information_id=125041&print=print

Kahn, L. & Smith, M.L. (2001, November 30). School choice policies in the political spectacle. *Education Policy Analysis Archives, 9*(50). Retrieved March 26, 2012, from http://epaa.asu.edu/epaa/v9n50.html

Martin, D. (2009, September 4). Teacher licensing revamp advances. *Fort Wayne News Sentinel.* Retrieved March 15, 2015, from http://www.news-sentinel.com/apps/pbcs.dll/article?AID=/20090904/NEWS/909040334

McFeely, D. (2010, January 8). Teachers may need a different major. *The Indianapolis Star.* Retrieved March 27, 2012, from http://www.indystar.com/article/20100108/NEWS04/1080384/Teachers-may-need-different-major

Merritt, D.B. & McCombs, M. E. (2014). *The two W's of journalism: the why and what of public affairs reporting.* New York, NY: Routledge.

Schneider, M.B. (2010, March 30). Daniels signs rules for teacher licensing. *The Indianapolis Star*. Retrieved March 12, 2012, from http://www.indystar.com/article/20100330/NEWS05/3300381

Smith, M.L. & Miller-Kahn, L. (2004). *Political spectacle and the fate of American schools.* New York, NY: Routledge.

Sleeter, C. (2008). Equity, democracy, and neoliberal assaults on teacher education. *Teaching and Teacher Education: An International Journal of Research and Studies, 24*(8), 1947-1957

Van Wyke, R. (2009, July 29). Indiana schools chief wants simpler teacher licensing. *WTHR.com.* Retrieved Sept. 20, 2013, from http://www.wthr.com/Global/story.asp?S=10808699

WXIN-TV. (2009, July 29). Simpler teacher licensing wanted by Indiana school chiefs. *Fox59.com.* Retrieved September 20, 2013, from http://www.fox59.com/wxin-simpler-teacher-license-wanted-072909,0,4371538.story

The Empowering Impacts of Chinese Social Media Weibo

John Yu Zhang

Abstract. The Internet has become the battleground between authorities and citizens in competing for the hearts and minds of the Chinese public (Qiang, 2011). In the meantime, the Internet has provided everyone with various "weapons," turning ordinary Chinese citizens into amateur reporters and news moderator, and rendering traditional censorship less meaningful and almost irrelevant. In the arsenal of the Internet, Weibo or microblog, which is the Chinese version of twitter, has a unique, sweeping, immediate and powerful effect on the Chinese society and public, often triggering some desired or undesired response and movement. This paper examines the impacts of the Chinese social media Weibo in the following areas: breaking the state information monopoly; empowering citizens' civic engagement; facilitating dissent, and becoming a watchdog for public good.

Keywords: China, Social Media, Weibo, Citizen Empowerment.

Introduction

China's persistent censorship has trained the Chinese citizens to not only become sensitive to official information but also eager for alternative sources of information (Sparks, 2010). Information on Weibo threatens of becoming political quicksand (Guo & Feng, 2012) that can undermine the carefully crafted facade of social harmony.

Weibo can snowball and shape public discussion of an otherwise usual event or incident into potent national dialogues. For example, in early 2013, a school principal spent a night in a hotel room with four underage girls in southern China's Hainan province. The furious citizens posted photographs of themselves on Weibo with the hand-held message: "Principal, get a room with me, leave the young students alone." The online public reaction has resulted in the quick firing, prosecution and sentencing of the principal to 13 years in prison, all within weeks (Xinhua News Agency, 2013, June 20). In another example, a Chinese teenager scratched "Ding Jinhao visited here" in Chinese on a temple wall in the ancient city of Luxor in May 2013. A posted photo triggered thousands of comments, lashing out at Ding and his act. The 15-year-old boy was quickly identified, prompting his parents to publicly apologize to the nation for damaging the image of the Chinese people (Associated Press, 2013, May 28).

The transparent and equalizing Weibo platform has undoubtedly empowered the average Chinese citizens with an unprecedented opportunity to expose any misconduct. Even the central government leverages the online exposures to help strengthen its supervision of officials (Yeo & Li, 2012; Tang, 2005). Such dynamics between the Chinese masses and the Chinese authorities has forged a socially vibrant environment (Cheong & Gong, 2010). The Chinese leadership, while continuing to view economic development as their first priority, now pays more attention to social injustice, inequality, economic disparities and public dissatisfactions (Taylor, 2012; Tang & Sampson, 2012). It is under these circumstances that Weibo provides an answer that the state and the public have been looking for.

Breaking the State Monopoly

In China's traditional media, the Party-state can easily control the information flow and information becomes a privilege for authorities but a luxury for common citizens (Shao, Lu & Wu, 2012). Traditional media content is subject to extensive editorial review and political monitoring. Even worse, Gu (2014) argued that due to the lack of alternative information channels, the Chinese could only passively succumb to the imposed messages from state media, which usually ignore citizens' concerns and complaints. Petitioning and appealing their cases or causes further are often cost prohibitive and emotionally difficult. Protesting on the street is generally not allowed or ignored. Overall, the basic right of expressing one's opinion or discontent is trampled.

Weibo and other social media, however, break such power and information asymmetry (Shao, Lu & Wu, 2012; Gu, 2014) and empower citizens to collect, report, analyse, disseminate and petition information via "citizen journalism" without having to seek approval from authorities (Han, 2011). In this regard, Weibo and other social media have become a public sphere to drive free information and speech. Weibo's rich media and threaded comments attract users to create, repost, and comment. Public discourse of all types, topics, styles, and persuasions have blossomed and flooded the social media (Leibold, 2011; Xu, 2012). Blocking the bursting information flood may not be as effective as diverting and guiding it. Furthermore, the citizens' online discourses have become so helpful that even the Chinese Communist Party (CCP) has begun to rely on them (Sullivan, 2012) to help catch corrupt officials and make policy changes.

Despite insisting on censorship, the Chinese government also plays a central role in driving the exponential growth of Chinese Internet, which helps break its own monopoly of information. According to the China Internet Network Information Centre survey, China had 3.2 million websites by the end of December 2013, a growth rate of 19.4% from 2012. The overall Chinese instant messaging users grew to 532 million, up by 64.4 million compared to the end of 2012 and with a utilization ratio of up to 86.2% (CNNIC, 2014).

There is, however, consensus over censorship between the Chinese masses and the Chinese government in the areas of pornography, rumour, fraud and violence. Particularly, malicious messages and software, such as rumours and computer viruses which cause harm for commercial or political purposes are seen as sabotaging social integrity. There is therefore little disagreement on cracking down on such information.

Promoting Civic Engagement

The Chinese government's long-time strategy of maximizing economic growth but minimizing sensitive information no longer works. Voices demanding free information, political reform and social justice are overwhelming, and the Chinese authorities must respond with real changes. The CCP's ultimate appeal, at home and abroad, while still resting largely on the country's economic success, now increasingly depends on making real progress in the areas of freedom of speech and political reform. The Chinese leadership is pushing information transparency so as to redistribute opportunities and resources to the long neglected, disadvantaged and marginalized populations and regions. The reform-minded CCP leadership is increasingly responsive to public demands and applies various strategies and campaigns to guide the masses to civic engagement. China's market-oriented Party propaganda helps stabilize the increasingly responsive authoritarianism (Stockmann, 2014) by allowing citizens to vent their frustrations on Weibo.

Guiding China's huge and growing well-informed and networked public toward "correct" information and thought is not easy. The openness brought by Weibo has allowed the Chinese public to become more outspoken and engaged in social, public and state affairs (Chiu, Ip & Silverman, 2012). Weibo enables and encourages users to upload and view posts along with photos, video, and web links in an attractive and user-friendly interface. Weibo forces co-governance and mutual supervision between the state and citizens (Gu, 2014) and empowers the Chinese 'netizens' to redefine government control toward guiding public opinion to reach a consensus between the government and the public.

Facilitating Dissent

Commercialization has motivated China's increasingly profit-driven media to provide what the public wants and report on controversial and sensitive topics (Stockmann & Gallagher, 2011). Media exposure often results in the overturn of unjust decisions and prompts investigation of corruption, inefficiency and waste. The only caveat is that while the state encourages the media to supervise local officials, it prohibits challenging the central government and top national leaders, projecting a "nice central but bad local" image to divert public resentment (Stockmann, 2014) toward corrupt officials rather than the CCP in general. The central government such as the State Council, the CCP Central Committee and the Politburo, and other politically significant institutions are usually shielded from negative coverage. The media still serve as a propaganda tool, portraying the top political institutions and leadership as righteous (Yang & Tang, 2010).

The growth of social media in general and Weibo in particular has provided the Chinese citizens with an unprecedented ability and opportunity to challenge the dominance of the state media. Citizens now have the freedom to discuss almost anything to a potentially unlimited audience. Without the limitation of time and space and with its global reach and open access, citizens can influence other people with no or little cost. Equally significant, the nature and feature of Weibo, to some extent, insulate the netizens and their messages from state censorship. Not only are the freedom and decision of posting and deleting messages resting solely with posters themselves (Gu, 2014), but the convenient, autonomous and interactive platform keeps citizens current on what is going on in real time. Weibo synergizes and combines individual voices to exert a powerful impact. As a public oasis for citizens to engage in social affairs and vent dissatisfactions, Weibo becomes a valuable source of public feedback on current social issues for the CCP, which helps improve the relations between the masses and the Party.

Weibo has boosted China's democratization by breaking down state information monopoly and providing citizens with more opportunities to express and share their opinions. However, the Weibo phenomena defied the prediction of Western observers who believed that information technology would compel China to adopt a western-style democracy (Hartford, 2000). In China, democracy thrives in a different form, when netizens' comments can help reconstruct and strengthen social and political accountability and enable direct engagement and open discussion on issues. The participatory and interactive nature of Weibo forces authorities to relax their censorship. Furthermore, the participation of amateur citizen "journalists" is forcing professional journalists to become competitive sense-makers instead of parrots of the Party lines.

A New Public Watchdog

Chinese President Xi Jinping has called corruption a fatal threat to the nation, society, and the Party, and a deviation from socialist values. Since Xi became the General Secretary of the CCP, the Party has been cracking down on both the corrupted 'flies' (low-ranking officials) at the bottom and the 'tigers' (high ranking officials) at the top. Both Chinese citizens and authorities are leveraging the Internet, especially Weibo, to demand local government agencies to enforce social justice, punish corrupt officials and improve their performance. The increasing awareness and exposure of corruption cases on Weibo have forced the Party leadership to widen, deepen and speed up the anti-corruption fight. In this sense, Weibo has become an anti-corruption partner and watchdog, linking the netizens who feed information and the CCP's disciplinary mechanisms that seek and use this information to fight corruption. To a certain degree, the Chinese citizens, the Party and Weibo are all partners in this campaign.

Information from Weibo has empowered ordinary Chinese citizens to monitor and challenge the government and officials by exposing the wrongdoings and amplifying the abuse of power (Cheong & Gong, 2010). The Chinese government also increasingly leverages Weibo to measure public opinion, test-drive policies and respond to citizens' concerns. As such, Weibo helps formulate a co-governing agreement between the Chinese authorities and the masses.

Through Weibo, Chinese netizens can satisfy their curiosities by receiving and feeding information and perspectives on diverse and sensitive issues. Weibo's multimedia formats add more interest and depth and allow readers to respond to postings and comments from other readers in a variety of ways. As such, netizens become active participants instead of passive readers. For example, Yang Dacai, a then Shaanxi provincial official, was often photographed wearing luxurious and brand watches, thus gaining the nickname 'Brother Watch'. In August 2012, when visiting the site of a serious traffic accident that killed 36 people, Yang was photographed smiling, which triggered heated reactions on Weibo, and resulted in more pictures of him wearing various luxurious watches on many occasions. The online outrage and unrest soon led to an official probe and his dismissal (Taylor 2012). In

September 2013, Yang was sentenced to 14 years in prison for bribery and possession of assets of unclear origin (China News Network, 2013, September 5).

As can be seen from the above analysis and example, a key reason that Weibo is popular in China is that the state can use it as a watchdog mechanism for the public good, while also allowing the Chinese population to vent their frustrations and report abuse.

Concluding Remarks

Social media in general and Weibo in particular contribute to the creation of new social and political forces in China, giving the Chinese people more freedom, rights and influence in decision making. This has led toan increasingly vibrant and transparent online environment and society, gradually shifting away from unilateral authoritarian control. Weibo and other social media have empowered the Chinese population, thus resulting in a new balance of power and a dwindling state monopoly on information while providing a channel for authorities to respond to public criticisms and requests.

References

Associated Press (2013, May 28). Chinese teen sparks outcry after writing name on Egyptian temple wall [Press release]. Retrieved March 30, 2015, from http://www.foxnews.com/world/2013/05/28/outcry-after-chinese-teen-defaces-ancient-egyptian-temple/

Cheong, H. & Gong, J. (2010). Cyber vigilantism, transmedia collective intelligence, and civic participation. *Chinese Journal of Communication, 3*(4), 471-487.

China News Network (2013, September 5). Yang Dacai sentenced to 14 years. Retrieved April 2, 2015 from http://www.chinanews.com/fz/2013/09-05/5248521.shtml

Chiu, C., Ip, C. & Silverman, A. (2012). Understanding social media in China. *McKinsey Quarterly*, April 2012, 1-4. Retrieved March 31, 2015, from http://www.mckinsey.com/insights/marketing_sales/understanding_social_media_in_china

CNNIC (2014) The 33rd China's Internet Development Report. Retrieved from http://www.cnnic.net.cn.

Gu, Q. (2014). Sina Weibo: A Mutual Communication Apparatus between the Chinese Government and Chinese Citizens. *China Media Research, 10* (2), 72-85.

Guo, S. & Feng, G. (2012). Understanding Support for Internet Censorship in China: An Elaboration of the Theory of Reasoned Action. *Journal of Chinese Political Science 17*(1), 33–52.

Han, H. (2011). Research on microblog in China's core Journals of Journalism and Communication. *China Media Report Overseas, 7*(3), 15-22.

Hartford, K (2000). Cyberspace with Chinese characteristics. *Current History, 99*(638), 255-262.

Leibold, J. (2011). Blogging alone: China, the Internet, and the democratic illusion? *The Journal of Asian Studies, 70* (4), 1023-1041.

Qiang, X. (2011). The battle for the Chinese Internet. *Journal of Democracy, 22*(2), 47-61.

Shao, G., Lu, J., & Wu, J. (2012). New media and civic engagement in China: The case of the Xiamen PX event. *China Media Research, 8*(2), 76-82.

Sparks, C. (2010). China's media in comparative perspective. *International Journal of Communication, 4*(2010), 552–566.

Stockmann, D. (2014). *Media Commercialization and Authoritarian Rule in China.* Cambridge University Press.

Stockmann, D. & Gallagher, M. E. (2011). Remote Control: how the media sustains authoritarian rule in China. *Comparative Political Studies, 44*(4), 436–467.

Sullivan, J. (2012). A tale of two microblogs in China. *Media Culture & Society, 34*(6), 774-783.

Tang, W. F. (2005). *Public Opinion and Political Change in China.* Stanford: Stanford University Press.

Tang, L. & Sampson, H. (2012). The interaction between mass media and the Internet in nondemocratic states: The case of China. *Media Culture and Society, 34* (4), 457-471.

Taylor, A. (2012). Chinese Official photographed smirking after a traffic accident that left 36 dead has been fired. *Business Insider.* Retrieved from http://www.businessinsider.com/

Xinhua News Agency (2013, June 20). Principle sentenced 13 years for checking into hotel room in Hainan with under-age girls.

Xu, Y.C. (2012). Understanding netizen discourse in China. *China Media Research, 8*(1).

Yang, Q. & Tang, W. F. (2010). Exploring the Sources of institutional Trust in China: Culture, Mobilization, or Performance? *Asian Politics and Policy, 2*(3), 415–436.

Yeo, G. & Li, E. (2012). Yin and Yang: Sina Weibo and the Chinese state. *New Perspective Quarterly*, 29(2), 7-9. Retrieved March 31, 2015, from http://digitalnpq.org/archive/2012_spring/02_yeo.html

Laughing while Learning: Using Comedic Reporting and Commentary in the Classroom

Sarah Attfield and Liz Giuffre

Abstract. This article explores the use of comedic reporting, commentary and fictional entertainment in higher education learning and teaching. Drawing on the success of infotainment and comedy news formats like *The Daily Show*, we suggest that a change in the way materials are delivered may help engage students who are not otherwise engaged. We offer a preliminary set of examples from our teaching in Australian universities where mainstream television, film and popular music has been used as teaching tools to spark student debate, interest and illuminate theory, comparing these experiences to existing literature about the function of these texts as genre pieces and new communication methods. We examine the use of these infotainment tools as ways to keep students' attention, but also acknowledge that these can be possible tools for distraction.

Keywords: Comedy, Media and Communications, Educational approaches, Infotainment

Introduction

Students in higher education currently have easy access to an unprecedented amount of information. This quantity of resources does not necessarily equate to quality. Students are often drawn to resources they uncover first rather than those selected using academic research strategies. Part of the problem is the usual delivery format of course materials – often appearing in exclusive publications and written with relatively dry jargon-heavy prose. The same issue also appears in face to face delivery of content, with teachers looking for ways to deliver material in an accessible way, but also with the necessary nuance required to professionally communicate complicated theoretical concepts and debate. We have regularly faced these issues as part of our experience teaching large groups of undergraduate students in media, communications and cultural studies courses over the last decade.

This article is a preliminary exploration into different ways of approaching complex content delivery in the classroom, particularly the problem of engaging relatively young students with otherwise 'difficult' or 'dry' materials. Our inquiry has been inspired by the success of new generation 'news' formats like Comedy Central's *The Daily Show*, an approach to content delivery which has been celebrated for being particularly effective in encouraging younger viewers to engage with otherwise difficult or dry content such as political debate (Becker, 2010; Feldman, 2007; Holbert, 2007). *The Daily Show*, in particular, has been credited with creating a change in the way audiences expect types of content to be delivered, or what Baym (2005) called a "reinvention of political journalism" (p.259), with some commentators suggesting now that its approach holds "traditional news accountable" (Painter, 2010, p.257). Similar claims have been made about international hybrid programs like *The Gruen Transfer* in Australia (Giuffre, 2013), as well as comparable examples from Europe, the Middle East and India (Baym and Jones, 2012). As Baym and Jones (2012) observe, there is a specific power in the combination of comedic address and 'serious' content, with "the power of news parody seem[ing] to lie in its portability [and] its ability to cross national, cultural, and linguistic boundaries" (p.8). While our problem is much smaller in scope (that is, we are aiming to gain and maintain the attention and interest of individual classroom groups or cohorts in the first instance), we are inspired by the versatility of this type of address. Modern universities should be places where a diverse student body gathers – as such, we seek to appeal to this diversity as effectively as possible.

We acknowledge that the delivery of communication in a higher education environment is a discrete discipline in itself, and as Chong and Arhmed (2015) put it, "Higher education [is] a service provider with unique challenges" (p.160). However we are confident in the lessons that can be learned by drawing on other successful communication modes in meeting the needs of higher education learners. It makes sense to approach teaching communication and media theory by using tactics that have been successfully employed by those who practice in those industries. This helps to ensure that content is relevant to contemporary industry standards, but also meets students where they begin in their learning careers – starting out as audiences of communication and media, and graduating as scholars and practitioners in the field. Given that the media is increasingly running commentary about the quality of higher education (Cabalin, 2014), we also feel this overview of current cross disciplinary literature is timely. We are wary of the need to consider 'substance' when delivering serious content in an apparently unserious way (Fox, 2007), however we do this by drawing on the existing literature which studies comedy as a 'serious art'. In particular, we note that comedy's marginalization in genre studies can often be attributed to political debates around audience value and worth rather than the communication skills of artists themselves, a problem of 'being taken seriously' that has plagued commentators of comedy from the time of Aristotle, who famously offered the provocation that comedy was merely an unmotivated opposite of tragedy, manifest as "an imitation of inferior people" (Heath, 1996, p. 9) rather than something that expressed a noble, dramatic pain. And later theorists such as Theodor Adorno and Max Horkheimer (2002) viewed comedy (especially in cinema) as the enemy of thought. They described fun as a "medicinal bath" that temporarily soothed the masses at the behest of the "pleasure industry" (p.112).

Understanding comedy as a form of communicating (and teaching)

We begin by examining comedy as a specific way of communicating. This in itself is a task that many commentators have tried to address, but few have been able to agree on. Stott (2003) argues that comedy "is a term that can refer equally to a genre, a tone, a series of effects that manifest themselves in diverse environments" (p.3), while King (2002) suggests that comedy can engage audiences in a variety of ways including as "a mode [of address], genre, adjective or noun" (p.3). King's work, which explores the machinations of specifically communicating with film, is useful for us here because it highlights the variety of ways comedy can draw audiences towards the artistic work – and by extension, we will suggest, the potential for drawing a variety of students towards engaging with complex curriculum.

We are also wary of King's (2003) warning that "comedy, by its definition, is not usually taken entirely seriously" (p.2). The issue of being taken seriously is one that has plagued educators who have tried to incorporate comedy into their practice in the past. In their review of four decades of research into humour and education, Banas et al (2011) observe that over this time there has been repeated need for "instructional communication scholars [to] address the relationship between [humour] and credibility" (p.130), observing that "generally, researchers have found instructor credibility to be related positively with appropriate instructional [humour] use" (Ibid., p.130). Garner's (2006) study into the impact of humour in the university classroom revealed that academic staff who used humour were generally highly rated in student evaluations which indicates the high value students place on an instructor's sense of humour and use of humorous materials. Garner (2006) found that students reported a "positive impact on content retention" (p.179) when appropriate humour was used and suggests that use of humour can provide a "cognitive break that allows the student to assimilate the information" (Ibid., p. 179) and potentially create new perspectives on the material presented.

Garner (2006) does warn though that humour needs to be used with caution due to the possibility of inappropriate content. What counts as 'appropriate use' is somewhat subjective. Methods of comedic delivery and use of humour have been examined by looking at language use by teachers (Generous, 2014), as well as the presentation of new purpose-made comedic teaching materials (Lupton, 2013) and the use of existing comedy artworks (Tewell, 2014). In each case there has been an argument for the benefits of using comedy in teaching, however "research findings are inconsistent in supporting how the use of humour in teaching is best achieved" (Struthers, 2011, p. 441). Importantly, comedy can help ensure the student experience is of a higher quality beyond the mere gaining of attention or sparking of interest. As Torok et al (2004) argue, "Students and faculty at all levels of education face a plethora of pressures, including, but hardly limited to, high stakes testing"(p.18), something they suggest can be alleviated by comedy as "humor appropriately used has the potential to humanize, illustrate, defuse, encourage, reduce anxiety, and keep people thinking, even given such pressures" (Ibid., p.18). However the link between the appropriate and inappropriate use remains one that needs to be carefully trodden. As explained by Wanzer et al (2006), at times the use of comedy in the same classroom can at once be considered in an "overlap between appropriate and inappropriate categories," (p. 194) a point they make by surveying students to find that at times "humor targeted at students was identified as both appropriate and inappropriate" (Ibid., p. 194).

While such findings might be considered initially confusing, they also confirm the complexity of dealing with comedy in the classroom – demonstrating that it may not be possible to match techniques for all students all the time, and that such an expectation should be perhaps shifted towards working with adaptable models. Context is important in whether something is perceived as funny, and it is possible that students simply will not 'get' the joke, or could find the humour offensive. Humour is a social interaction and often requires a shared social or cultural context to be understood (Cheng, 2003). While it might not be possible to find a humorous example that all students will find funny, the instructor should be mindful of the humour used and try to ensure that the risk of offense is minimal. This is particularly the case when employing sarcasm, which, according to Torok et al (2004), can be used "effectively and constructively"(p.18) if it is non-hostile in nature and used in a classroom where a good rapport between students and instructor has already been established.

Comedy in learning and teaching practice: some examples

Methods of 'reading' comedic material have been widely circulated in and beyond education and media and communications literature. Speck's

"Humorous Message Taxonomy" (1991) has been widely used as way of exploring comedy and advertising, and comedic practitioners and academics such as Australian writer/performer/producer/academic Tim Ferguson (2010) have written narrative comedy textbooks designed for those wanting to produce, as well as understand, comedy as a type of communication.

We offer something slightly different to the examples above – a way of working backwards to use comedy to study other forms of communications methods and theory. This is not without precedent, with one of the most obvious examples being the "Popular Culture and Philosophy" series by Open Court Publishing. This series has published eighty eight edited collections, including, notably, one dedicated to *The Daily Show[1]*. The use of materials that are widely accessible but curated by us as teachers is different insofar as we seek to invite students to draw on comedic examples to help them understand concepts, but we also ensure that students understand that the examples are used as illustrations of concepts and do not substitute for academic explanations.

In first year undergraduate communications and media theory subjects we have attempted to illustrate ideas through humorous examples. These include examples from classic British comedy such as Monty Python as well as more current contemporary materials from satirists such as John Oliver. British satirist John Oliver's 2014 package "Newscasters Misidentifying Photographs as Selfies"[2] on his *Last Week Tonight* show offers a very basic reminder of the need to define terms and test them against the given criteria. The package draws attention to the 'truth' – these are authority figures (in the media) who apparently are unable to follow very basic rules. If the outcome as an audience is that we lose confidence in the argument, the same basic lesson can be applied to tasks in the classroom -- the need to apply and test a definition, or risk the viewer/reader (marker) losing confidence in the student's ability.

The 1969 "Dead Parrot Sketch"[3] from *Monty Python's Flying Circus* has been used to illustrate the phenomenological approach to communication theory – the sketch centres around contradictory perceptions of a parrot which illustrates very well the ways in which reality and perception are influenced by experience. While the humour in this sketch is absurd in nature, it also demonstrates to students how writers incorporate theories into their work.

---

[1] Information taken from http://www.opencourtbooks.com/categories/pcp.htm, accessed 5/3/15

[2] https://www.youtube.com/watch?v=oHNx2VVDDnE

[3] https://www.youtube.com/watch?v=4vuW6tQ0218

This is important in the context of our university courses which place a strong emphasis on the blending of theory and (professional) practice.

A rather more direct example has been used in the presentation of ideas on race and white privilege. Australian comedy duo, Aamer Rahman and Nazeem Hussain, who collectively are known as *Fear of a Brown Planet*, present insightful stand-up routines on topics such as white privilege, racism and Islamaphobia. Aamer Rahman's routine "Workshop for Whitey"[4] deals with the ways in which white people communicate with people of colour and highlights the subtle and often insidious ways that racism occurs. Rahman's routine is funny, but there is a serious and political message and the video is quite impactful. White students have informed us that they find the issues raised in this and other routines educational and they report on how the material has challenged their previous understandings of racism. Students of colour have indicated that the videos are empowering because their experiences are validated within the routines.

We also use material from *The Gruen Transfer* (an Australian television show that analyses advertising and marketing campaigns in a humorous way) to illustrate issues around ethics in advertising. There are other comedy sketches that are useful in discussions around language, such as the British comedy duo, Armstrong and Miller's 2007-2010 series of sketches on the origins of various forms of communication such as small talk. Other sketches provide material on inter-textuality and incongruity (again, Armstrong and Miller are useful here, particularly their sketches involving two recurring characters – World War II fighter pilots who appear in scenes that resemble British World War II studio films, but who, despite their clichéd 'plummy' British accents, use contemporary British youth colloquial grammar and slang).

British comedian Catherine Tate's characters such as "Posh Mum" provide a humorous way into discussions of class and communication and the 1990s Australian sketch show *Full Frontal* includes a sketch devoted to bad cutaways[5] which is useful as an instructional 'what not to do' tool for students asked to produce filmed interviews for assignments. Australian satirical comedy shows such as *The Chaser* (1999-2005) provide useful segments for discussions around media practice, media ethics and politics.

---

[4] https://www.youtube.com/watch?v=uuDvAInMYgU
[5] https://www.youtube.com/watch?v=Ix-G3Nz8Tow

Conclusions about laughing while learning

Comedy is unquestionably a valuable tool for communicating difficult ideas, and for facilitating a relaxed and friendly atmosphere in the classroom. While some instructors might maintain a humorous tone throughout their classes, others create this atmosphere through the selection of humorous materials relating to the topics being taught. There are pitfalls to using humour in this way, and it could be suggested that humour could be a distraction or might deflect from serious issues being discussed. But if used carefully, with the understanding that context is important for the appreciation of humour, students can learn while laughing and find the experience much richer as a result.

References

Adorno, Theodor and Horkheimer, Max (trans Edmund Jephcott) (2002) *Dialectic of Enlightenment: Philosophical Fragments*, Stanford: Stanford University Press.

Aristotle (trans Malcolm Heath) (1996): *Poetics*, Penguin Books, London.

Banas, John A; Dunbar, Norah; Rodriguez, Dariela & Liu, Shr-Jie (2011): "A Review of Humor in Educational Settings: Four Decades of Research", *Communication Education*, 60(1), 115-144.

Baym, Geoffrey (2005): "The Daily Show: Discursive Integration and the Reinvention of Political Journalism", *Political Communication*, 22(3), 259-276.

Baym, Geoffrey and Jones, Jeffery P (2012): "News Parody in Global Perspective: Politics, Power, and Resistance", *Popular Communication*, 2012, 10(1-2), 2-13.

Becker, Amy B (2010): "Sizing Up: Audience Perceptions of Political Comedy Programming", *Atlantic journal of communication*, 18(3), 144-157.

Cabalin, Cristian (2014): "Mediatizing higher education policies: discourses about quality education in the media", *Critical Studies in Education*, 1-19.

Cheng, Winnie (2003): "Humor in Intercultural Conversations", *Semiotica*, 146(1/4), 287 – 306.

Chong, Yit Sean & Ahmed, Pervaiz K. (2015): "Student motivation and the 'feel good' factor: an empirical examination of motivational predictors of university service quality evaluation", *Studies in Higher Education*, 40(1), 158-177.

Day, Amber (2011) *Satire and Dissent: Interventions in Contemporary Political Debate*, Bloomington: Indiana University Press.

Feldman, Lauren (2007): "The news about comedy: Young audiences, The Daily Show, and evolving notions of journalism", *Journalism*, 8(4), 406-427.

Ferguson, Tim (2010): *The Cheeky Monkey: Writing Narrative Comedy*, Currency Press, Melbourne.

Fox, Julia (2007): "No Joke: A Comparison of Substance in and Broadcast Network Television Coverage of the 2004 Presidential Election Campaign", *Journal of broadcasting & electronic media*, 51(2), 213-227.

Garner, R.L. (2006): "Humor in Pedagogy: How Ha-Ha Can Lead to Aha!", *College Teaching*, 54(1), 177-180.

Generous, Mark A; Frei, Seth S. & Houser, Marian L. (2014): "When an Instructor Swears in Class: Functions and Targets of Instructor Swearing from College Students' Retrospective Accounts", *Communication Reports*, 1-13.

Giuffre, Liz (2013): "Pitch perfect: The growth of 'Gruen' and the case for serious entertainment", *Metro Magazine: Media & Education Magazine*, 176, 106-110.

Gray, Jonathon (2009) *Satire: TV Politics and Comedy in the Post-Network Era*, New York: NYU Press.

Holbert, R Lance (2007): "Primacy Effects of and National TV News Viewing: Young Viewers, Political Gratifications, and Internal Political Self-Efficacy", *Journal of broadcasting & electronic media*, 51(1), 20-38.

King, Geoff (2002): *Film Comedy*, Wallflower Press, London.

Lupton, Mandy (2013): "Reclaiming the art of teaching", *Teaching in Higher Education*, 18(2), 156-166.

Mera, Miguel (2002): "Is Funny Music Funny?: Contexts and case studies of film music humour", *Journal of Popular Music Studies*, 14(2), 91- 113.

Speck, Paul Surgi (1991): "The Humorous Message Taxonomy: A Framework for the Study of Humorous Ads", *Current Issues and Research in Advertising*, 13(1-2), 1-44.

Stott, Andrew (2006): *Comedy*, Routledge, New York

Struthers, John (2011): "The case for mixed methodologies in researching the teacher's use of humour in adult education", *Journal of Further and Higher Education*, 35(4), 439-459.

Tewell, Eamon C. (2014): "Tying Television Comedies to Information Literacy: A Mixed-Methods Investigation", *The Journal of Academic Librarianship*, 40, 134-141.

Torok, SE, McMorris, RE and Lin, WC (2004): "Is humor an appreciated teaching tool? Perceptions of Professors' teaching styles and uses of humor", *College Teaching*, 52(1), 14-20.

Wanzer, Melissa Bekelja; Frymier, Ann Bainbridge; Wojtaszczyk, Ann M. & Smith, Tony (2006): "Appropriate and Inappropriate Uses of Humor by Teachers", *Communication Education* 55(2), 178-196.

Social Media in the Classroom

Stephanie Sadownik

Abstract. Many educators choose not to participate on social media websites. I believe this is due to the lack of rules in online environments, leaving an impression that they are unpredictable and uncontrollable. It is also apparent that respectful engagement is not always the case on social media websites. Trust and privacy issues thus counter the freedom offered by social media. This impression may have an impact on how educators approach incidents of cyber-bullying. I believe that anti-bullying campaigns and education offered in schools would be more effective if educators integrated digital citizenship with the aid of social media into their daily classroom lives.

Keywords: social constructions of knowledge, curriculum design, social media.

Introduction

I have a theory. It is an emerging conceptual development of what I believe education is for and what it could be. My theory is based on the premise that children are constantly constructing knowledge based on their environment and the discourse they are surrounded by; this discourse is not limited to face-to-face interactions. Today's discourse is a combination of real and virtual worlds that intertwine in students' lives and cross boundaries of formalities between what is acceptable behaviour and what is not. I also believe that left to their own devices, students form understandings of society based on the discourses they are exposed to and the reaction of others while they witness this discourse. Egan (2003) notes that, "in all human societies, children are initiated into particular modes of making sense of their experience and the world about them" (p. 9).

Foundational curriculum figures such as John Dewey and Jean Jacques Rousseau celebrated the exploration of the child as a natural phenomenon and criticized a more stringent approach that limited their ability to learn from their own experiences. This curriculum argument has continued into the 21st century with a long standing debate of what should be taught and how. Although it has become universally acknowledged that students require skills regarding digital citizenship and the ethical use of technology, a clear understanding of how that should be taught is still under review. What I am proposing is a radical curriculum design that embraces the use of social media in the classroom and places the problematic discourse under a microscope for dissection and discussion with the teacher as the mediator and facilitator. Egan (2003) suggests that "to know what the curriculum should contain requires a sense of what the contents are for" (p. 14). In this paper, it is assumed that the purpose of education is twofold: primarily to keep students safe, and secondly to prepare them to live in the real world. Beauchamp (1982) suggests curriculum theorists have a job. It is to "describe the set of events, or phenomena, with which they are concerned in their work" (p. 24) and then purposefully and whole heartedly seek out and attack problems that are complicated by "searching out relationships among the phenomena and relationships among the relationships" (Ibid., p. 24). My theory is based on this premise. I am concerned about student abilities to understand social networking relationships and social media in general.

Social construction of knowledge, "is a direct reflection of Vygotsky (1978) sociocultural theory of learning" (Applefield, Huber, & Moallem, 2000, p. 38). It is devised from the notion that knowledge is constructed through social interactions, and these interactions allow individuals to "refine their own meanings and help others find meanings" (Applefield et. al., 2000, p. 38). In the case of social media, students are constructing knowledge as they witness events and discourse streaming down their computer screen. I propose as educators we have the opportunity to allow them to experience this within the safety of our classroom, and furthermore, we allow students to engage in a discussion about what is occurring. In so doing, we, as educators, help to monitor their social constructions of knowledge and have the opportunity to re-phrase, redirect or offer alternative perspectives when complex situations arise.

Building Community in the Classroom

One of the benefits associated with using collaborative work in classrooms is the possibility of also building knowledge communities (Scardamalia, 2002; Slotta & Najafi, 2013). The idea of building communities of knowledge became of interest last century, but now, in the 21st century, encompasses the use of Web 2.0 technologies (Slotta et. al., 2013). If social media is seen as a Web 2.0 technology, and collaborative discussions emerge regarding what students witness online, the use of social media in the classroom could potentially help to build knowledge communities as well.

Terwel (1999) suggests that "radical constructivism in education" (p. 198) may fail if the challenges faced when attempting to acquire knowledge are not overcome; these challenges are attributed to "prejudices, naïve concepts, misconceptions, subjectivism, solipsism and uncommitted relativism" (Ibid., p. 198). Using social media in the classroom, followed by group discussions, allows students to challenge their perceptions and beliefs by forcing students to rationalize their thinking.   Additionally, the classroom environment encourages students to work collaboratively, to discuss their thoughts and actions, to monitor and occasionally challenge each other's behaviour. In fact the importance of discussing the behaviour in the moment and environment in which it occurs is of the utmost importance. Pontecorvo (1993) relates to Bruner (1966) when he states, "cognitive development, in its overall definition, cannot even be interpreted outside a culture, i.e., outside the emotional, educational, and social mediations which make it possible" (Pontecorvo, 1993, p. 295).

In order to construct knowledge from social interactions, it is necessary to question, challenge, inquire, reason and explain thinking and/or actions. The justification of behaviour and thought has been shown to be a "crucial tool for learning to reason and to explain" (Ibid. p. 293). Social interactions between children reveal much more than their thinking; they also reveal their emotions and situate each learner within their own personal contexts. Beyond this, as students begin to contribute to the discussion, both support and opposition arise. Pontecorvo believes it is important to consider the "role of disagreement in classroom discussions" (Pontecorvo, 1993, p. 301). His findings provided evidence that "oppositional interaction supports children's efforts to produce 'good' arguments" (Ibid., p. 301-302).   One reason attributed to this development is related to students expanding on their thoughts, and providing examples or evidence that supported their argument in an effort to persuade others.

What it Means to be Human

What does it mean to be human? The answer to this question inevitably involves the making of mistakes, and encompasses various interactions with others in our environment. What does it mean to be intelligent? A common phrase that exemplifies this thought would be that insanity is doing the same thing over and over again and expecting different results; therefore, one might suggest intelligence is developed when one learns from their mistakes.

Gamification is a recent development in education that exemplifies this belief (Brown & Thomas, 2011). Curriculum theorists and reformers such as John Seely Brown and Douglas Thomas, are suggesting when students learn curriculum as though it was a video game, they learn to adapt and change their methods in order to advance to the next level. Related to this idea, is one of task persistence, since students are driven to attempt levels repeatedly until they have mastered the skills needed to advance. In one meta-analysis of learning interventions for low achievers, success was related to the combination of peer tutors and task persistence (Baker, Gersten, & Lee, 2002). Another study claimed developing "relational equity" helped students to work together and achieve more success than simply working together without it (Boaler, 2008). Conclusions can be drawn from these claims that when students work together, relate to each other, and show task persistence, they increase their intelligence.

A review of Kincheloe (2003) supports both of these views. He believes to be educated involves personal transformation. Therefore, one could surmise he believes the purpose of school is "to realize that the nature of the interactions in which the self engages actually changes the structure of the mind" (p. 48), and with this education it is imperative "to act on self and world in a just and an intelligent manner" (Ibid., p. 48).

Historically speaking, many curricular theorists have already laid the foundation to support the use of social media in the classroom through their experience-centred, humanistic and radical curriculum designs. John Dewey believed that children "exist in a personal world of experiences" (Ornstein & Hunkins, 2013, p. 166) and that their "spontaneous power -- their demand for self-expression -- cannot be suppressed" (Ibid., p. 166). Furthermore, Dewey believed children's educators should analyse experiences, since it was these experiences that shaped their knowledge.

Additionally, Ornstein & Hunkins (2013) refer to both Jürgen Habermas and Carl Rogers as being two prominent curriculum theorists. Specifically, radical constructivists draw from Jürgen Habermas who believed teachers are "awareness makers" (p. 167), who "emphasize that education's goal is emancipation of the awareness's, competencies, and attitudes that people need to take control of their lives" (Ibid., p. 167). Humanistic curriculum designers relate to Carl Rogers who suggested educating students in environments that encourage "genuineness, empathy, and respect for self and others" (Ibid., p. 168); further stating that "individuals able to initiate action and take responsibility are capable of intelligent choice and self-direction, where mistakes are accepted as part of the learning process" (Ibid., p. 168). The idea of blending feelings with knowledge emerged in the 1970's with the notion of "confluence education" (Ibid., p. 169) a combination of both affective and cognitive domains.

This type of learning and teaching is not without challenges. One of the most obvious would appear to be the ability of an educator to fill the multiple roles I have outlined above. While some facilitators may feel comfortable with an intellectual approach, many would shy away from being a moral, spiritual or emotional leader for their students. The objective relationship that helped to remove any blurring of lines between teachers and students, helped to keep political and religious agendas and backgrounds out of the educational movement of the 21st century. However, is it necessary to paint a completely black and white picture of the role of an educator in today's classrooms? How do we, as educators, facilitate change or help students to navigate real world problems if we are unwilling to wade into the water with them?

Conclusion

Many educators choose not to participate on social media websites. I believe this is due to the lack of rules in online environments, leaving an impression that they are unpredictable and uncontrollable. It is also apparent that respectful engagement is not always the case on social media websites. Trust and privacy issues thus counter the freedom offered by social media. This impression may have an impact on how educators approach incidents of cyber-bullying. I believe that anti-bullying campaigns and education offered in schools would be more effective if educators integrated digital citizenship with the aid of social media into their daily classroom lives. Furthermore, I believe this approach to teaching requires teachers to step into an uncomfortable area, where real world problems and emotions intertwine, but where the possibility of truly making a difference in students' lives can be found.

References

Applefield, J. M., Huber, R., & Moallem, M. (2000). Constructivism in theory and practice: Toward a better understanding. *The High School Journal*, 35-53.

Baker, S., Gersten, R., & Lee, D. S. (2002). A synthesis of empirical research on teaching mathematics to low-achieving students. *The Elementary School Journal*, 51-73.

Beauchamp, G. A. (1982). Curriculum theory: Meaning, development, and use. *Theory into practice*, *21*(1), 23-27.

Boaler, J. (2008). Promoting 'relational equity' and high mathematics achievement through an innovative mixed- ability approach. *British Educational Research Journal*, *34*(2), 167-194.

Thomas, D., & Brown, J. S. (2011). *A new culture of learning: Cultivating the imagination for a world of constant change* (Vol. 219). Lexington, KY: CreateSpace.

Bruner, J. S. (1966). On cognitive growth II. *Studies in cognitive growth*, 1-67.

Egan, K. (2003). What is curriculum? *Journal of the Canadian Association for Curriculum Studies, 1*(1), 9-16.

Kincheloe, J. L. (2003). Critical ontology: Visions of selfhood and curriculum. *Journal of Curriculum Theorizing, 19*(1), 47-64.

Ornstein, A.C., & Hunkins, F. P. (2013). *Curriculum: Foundations, principles, and issues*. Boston: Pearson.

Pontecorvo, C. (1993). Social interaction in the acquisition of knowledge. *Educational Psychology Review, 5*(3), 293-310.

Puntambekar, S. (2006). Analyzing collaborative interactions: divergence, shared understanding and construction of knowledge. *Computers & Education, 47*(3), 332-351.

Scardamalia, M. (2002). Collective cognitive responsibility for the advancement of knowledge. *Liberal education in a knowledge society, 97*, 67-98.

Slotta, J. D., & Najafi, H. (2013). Supporting collaborative knowledge construction with Web 2.0 technologies. In *Emerging Technologies for the Classroom* (pp. 93-112). Springer New York.

Terwel, J. (1999). Constructivism and its implications for curriculum theory and practice. *Journal of curriculum studies, 31*(2), 195-199.

Vygotsky, L.S. (1978). *Mind in society: The development of higher psychological processes*. (M. Cole, V. John-Steiner, S.Scribner & E. Souberman, Eds. and Trans.). Cambridge, MA: Harvard University Press.

Bringing Rape Culture Media into the Classroom

Diana C. Direiter

Abstract. Examples of Rape Culture can be found in most aspects of American media, but these examples are difficult to examine through traditional scholarship. Utilising the popular press and mainstream media allows for more immediate study of social phenomena and attitudes regarding Rape Culture. Additionally, examining and analysing memes, comments in social media and other examples of media, students are better able to connect the theoretical concepts of Rape Culture to their real life experiences, thus deepening their levels of integration and understanding.

Keywords: Rape culture; social media

Introduction

Although the term 'Rape Culture' is not new, American society has recently refocused on the concept. Rape cases that may or may not have been high profile on their own become part of a national conversation when they are associated with a Rape Culture viewpoint. One notable example is the 2012 rape case in Steubenville, Ohio, in which an inebriated and unconscious high school girl was sexually assaulted by 2 male classmates, both of whom were on the high school football team. Although the victim had no recollection of what had happened to her, multiple pictures of her assault had been shared on social media, some with commentary by the perpetrators. Aspects of this case that highlighted multiple issues related to Rape Culture included the boys' seeming lack of understanding of the nature of the crimes they were committing, allegations that coaches and other school officials attempted to cover up the rapes to protect the football team, and the role that social media played in how the assaults were widely broadcast among the adolescents, then soon discovered and investigated. Public opinion ranged from outrage at the teens and adults involved to blaming the victim for being too drunk to protect herself (Levy, 2013). Additionally, some of the media outlets covering the story were accused of perpetuating a Rape Culture for disclosing the victim's name or expressing a sympathy toward the perpetrators (Fung, 2013). This case, and others like it, has relevance to multiple academic areas including Criminal Justice, Communications, Adolescent Development, Women's

Studies, Journalism and Psychology. To date, however, there have been no peer-reviewed articles that have examined it.

Rape Culture influences in both implicit and explicit ways, but there is little opportunity to examine these messages through the lens of traditional scholarship. This paper discusses the benefits of using examples from media and social media in the classroom in order to capitalise on the immediacy of the public's responses as well as the ephemeral nature of these responses.

Rape Culture

First used in the 1970s, the term Rape Culture was one coined by feminists in an attempt to bring the prevalence of rape in American women's experience to light (Rutherford, 2011). Over time, the definition has broadened to describe an environment in which attitudes about unwanted sexual activity are tolerated, if not encouraged. As Emilie Buchwald described in *Transforming Rape Culture* (1995), rape culture is embodied in a society where "violence is seen as sexy and sexuality is violent" (p. v). Many feminist scholars, writers, activists and media critics who view America as being steeped in these beliefs, claim that the attitudes are disseminated and reinforced through jokes, movies, TV shows, and advertising, among other avenues (Maxwell, 2014; Friedman & Valenti, 2008; Chemaly, 2012) and claim that by normalising rape-related images and concepts, society becomes desensitised to them, contributing to an environment that then accepts rape itself. Elements of Rape Culture include victim-blaming, empathising with rapists or alleged rapists, perpetuation of rape myths (e.g., that false rape allegations are a common in response to regret about having had sex), general objectification of women and minimisation of the extent or effects of rape (Maxwell, 2014).

There are others who assert, however, that the concept of Rape Culture is a feminist attempt to portray women as perpetually victimised by men (Hoff Sommers, 2014). Still others see the popularised version of Rape Culture as being overly focused on a narrow and extreme aspect of violence (Kay, 2014) that is not actually reflected in the larger culture.

Although Rape Culture is not specific to college campuses, there have been a number of campus-based situations in which the dynamics are particularly evident. College sports teams and fraternities are often accused of being egregious perpetuators of college Rape Culture. Their emphasis on group conformity (Huchting, et al, 2011) -- particularly the conformity to stereotyped masculine norms (Steinfeldt, et al, 2011) – can breed an atmosphere in which sexual entitlement can run unchecked (Hill & Fisher, 2001).

As the number of colleges and universities under investigation for Title IX violations has almost doubled since May 2014 (Anderson, 2014; Kadveny, 2015) there has been increased attention brought to campus sexual assaults and some universities' inadequate responses to them. In 2014, *The White House* launched the "It's On Us" multimedia initiative to address this issue and a report by *The White House Council on Women and Girls* acknowledged, "sexual assault is pervasive because our culture still allows it to persist" (p. 9).

Mainstream Media vs. Academia

The 'ivory tower' mindset of higher education has long held that students should be immersed solely in the theoretical or historical realms of various disciplines. While there is, indeed, need for students to know the history and foundational aspects of their fields of study, the current culture is one that is proliferated and communicated through media.

Social media, in particular, is immediately responsive to news events of any scale. Although there seems to be an interpersonal disconnection that may be widening as the dependence on technology deepens (Turkle, 2012), there is also a democratic aspect of social media that quickly offers a collective voice in response to shared events. Applications such as *Twitter* have been credited with illuminating global atrocities as well as influencing political systems (Blair, 2013). It has also given the public the ability to instantaneously give commentary on a politician's gaffe (e.g., Romney's 2012 "binders full of women"), poke fun at a musical performance (e.g., Katy Perry's "Left Shark" dancer in her February 2015 Superbowl Halftime show) or explore scientific differences in perception (e.g., "The Dress" from March 2015).

Often, these moments of shared focus are immediate and intense, but extremely brief as another gaffe, performance, or event, quickly replaces the one preceding it. The time span marked by a particular element of the zeitgeist has been compressed from years to weeks, if not days. The connecting effect of these individual moments cannot be sustained for the length of time necessary to examine them with a traditional approach of academic rigor.

A March 2015 search in *Academic Search Premier* for articles in peer-reviewed journals with the key phrase "Rape Culture", resulted in 27 articles, 8 of which focused on rapeseed oil and honeybees. The same search terms with Google yielded 15,000,000 results. Results included links to definitions of rape culture, domestic and international news stories about it, sites that directly address it, protests about it, documentaries about it, sites to buy books about it and related social media forums including *YouTube, Tumblr, Facebook, Twitter* and *Instagram*. Although the options seem limitless, careful vetting of examples, resources and perspectives found in mainstream media enable faculty to teach the foundational information, while simultaneously making it relevant to students' lives. To rely exclusively on scholarly journals or historical text, especially in an area such as Rape Culture that is only now growing in society's collective consciousness, would eliminate virtually all examination of this concept.

There are also times that a piece of popular media benefits from that initial burst of immediacy, but invites ongoing participation by encouraging multiple perspectives and having a connection to a larger issue. In the 2014 Isla Vista murders, Elliot Rodgers attacked 20 individuals with a knife, gun or car, ultimately killing 6 of them, before committing suicide (CNN, 2014). He had made a video of himself describing his plan and detailing his hatred of women and desire to punish them for not being sexually interested in him. Although it had already been in use, the hashtag #NotAllMen became popular as many tried to make the point that Rodgers' beliefs and behaviours did not reflect those of all men. In response, another hashtag, #YesAllWomen, was created (Feeney, 2014). It became associated with comments suggesting that all women had an increased need for caution and protection, despite the fact that the perpetrators were only some of the men.

Although the original event has long passed, the hashtags remain in use and the conversation continues. A similar case, though less directly related to Rape Culture, involves the #WhyDoesn'tSheLeave and #WhyIStayed hashtags that came shortly after the widespread viewing of a video of an NFL football player, Ray Rice, hitting his female partner in an elevator, and then dragging her unconscious body out of it (Grinberg, 2014).

In the Fall of 2014, a female student at Columbia University began carrying her dorm mattress with her in protest of what she felt was the university's mishandling of her allegations of rape against another student. Using it as her senior art thesis, she named the performance art "Carry That Weight" and said that her mattress represented the emotional weight she had carried since she had been assaulted two years earlier (Barness, 2014). In addition to stories from traditional news outlets, a *Facebook* page was created, as were a website, a *Tumblr* blog and multiple videos on *Vimeo, Vine* and *Youtube*. All were tagged with #carrythatweight. A movement evolved in which students from other campuses began taking and posting pictures of themselves with mattresses or pillows with that hashtag to raise awareness of the issue as well as show solidarity with the student (Schonfeld, 2014).

By not only discussing current events, but also utilising essays from the popular press as well as examining memes and comments from social media, students are better able to integrate concepts related to rape culture. As online comments typically include an extreme range of reactions to issues related to Rape Culture, students are also given the opportunity to observe a microcosm of society and to consider multiple examples of hostility, cognitive dissonance, persuasion and misogyny.

Conclusion

Integrating the 'real world' into the classroom allows students to find immediate relevance to academic concepts. The material related to Rape Culture, in particular, has potential bearing on campus life as well as to larger societal, if not global, issues. Encouraging students to recognise and respond to examples of Rape Culture in their own academic community can lead to stronger student activism and advocacy for self and others. In fact, this author has had multiple experiences in which students note that exposure to and exploration of the concepts in the classroom led them to recognise the elements of Rape Culture in various media. Broadening the options of teaching materials to include resources that are immediate, accessible and familiar allows educators to guide students toward discovering, recognising and critiquing the often contradictory messages given to -- and received by – these emerging adults.

References

Anderson, N. (2014, October 19). *Tally of federal probes of colleges on sexual violence grows 50 percent since May*. Retrieved March 30, 2015, from http://www.washingtonpost.com/local/education/tally-of-federal-probes-of-colleges-on-sexual-violence-grows-50-percent-since-may/2014/10/19/b253f02e-54aa-11e4-809b-8cc0a295c773_story.html

Barness, S. (2014, September 3). *Columbia University Student Will Drag Her Mattress Around Campus Until Her Rapist Is Gone*. Retrieved March 31, 2015, from http://www.huffingtonpost.com/2014/09/03/emma-sulkowicz-mattress-rape-columbia-university_n_5755612.html

Blair, A. (2013). Democratising the Learning Process: The Use of Twitter in the Teaching of Politics and International Relations. *Politics, 33*(2), 135-145.

Buchwald, E., Fletcher, P., and Roth. M. (eds.) (1995). *Transforming Rape Culture*. Minneapolis: Milkweed Editions.

Chemaly, S. (2012, January 6). *Rape Culture: Men, Women, and Power*. Retrieved March 29, 2015, from http://goodmenproject.com/gender-sexuality/rape-culture-men-women-power/

Feeney, N. (2014, May 25). *The Most Powerful #YesAllWomen Tweets*. Retrieved March 30, 2015, from http://time.com/114043/yesallwomen-hashtag-santa-barbara-shooting/

Friedman, J., & Valenti, J. (2008). *Yes Means Yes!: Visions Of Female Sexual Power And A World Without Rape*. Berkeley: Seal Press.

Fung, K. (2013, March 18). *CNN, Fox News, MSNBC Air Name Of Steubenville Rape Victim*. Retrieved March 29, 2015, from http://www.huffingtonpost.com/2013/03/18/fox-news-steubenville-rape-victim_n_2901635.html

Grinberg, E. (2014, September 17). *Meredith Vieira explains #WhyIStayed*. Retrieved March 30, 2015, from http://www.cnn.com/2014/09/09/living/rice-video-why-i-stayed/

Hill, M. S., & Fischer, A. R. (2001). Does Entitlement Mediate the Link Between Masculinity and Rape-Related Variables? *Journal Of Counseling Psychology*, *48*(1), 39.

Hoff Sommers, C. (2014, May 15*). Rape Culture is a 'Panic Where Paranoia, Censorship, and False Accusations Flourish'* Retrieved March 29, 2015, from http://time.com/100091/campus-sexual-assault-christina-hoff-sommers/

Huchting, K. K., Lac, A., Hummer, J. F., & LaBrie, J. W. (2011). Comparing Greek-Affiliated Students and Student Athletes: An Examination of the Behavior-Intention Link, Reasons for Drinking, and Alcohol-Related Consequences. *Journal Of Alcohol & Drug Education*, *55*(3), 61-81.

Kadveny, E. (2015, March 4). *Office for Civil Rights opens sexual-assault investigation at Stanford University*. Retrieved March 30, 2015, from http://www.paloaltoonline.com/news/2015/03/04/office-for-civil-rights-opens-sexual-assault-investigation-at-stanford-university

Kay, B. (2014, March 8). *Barbara Kay: 'Rape culture' fanatics don't know what a culture is*. Retrieved March 29, 2015, from http://news.nationalpost.com/2014/03/08/barbara-kay-rape-culture-fanatics-dont-know-what-a-culture-is/

Levy, A. (2013, August 5). *Trial By Twitter - The New Yorker*. Retrieved March 31, 2015, from http://www.newyorker.com/magazine/2013/08/05/trial-by-twitter

Mass killing all too familiar in scenic college town of Isla Vista - CNN.com. (2014, May 27). Retrieved March 29, 2015, from http://www.cnn.com/2014/05/24/us/santa-barbara-isla-vista-shooting-profile/

Maxwell, Z. (2014). What you need to know about rape culture. *Essence, 45*(7), 78-78. Rutherford, A. (2011).   Sexual Violence Against Women.   *Psychology of Women Quarterly, 35(2).* Thousand Oaks, CA: Sage Publishing.

Schonfeld, Z. (2014, October 30). *Hundreds of Columbia Students Carry Mattresses in   Sexual   Assault   Protest.*   Retrieved   March   31,   2015,   from http://www.newsweek.com/photos-hundreds-columbia-students-carry-mattresses-sexual-assault-protest-280914

Steinfeldt, J. A., Halterman, A. W., Gomory, A., Gilchrist, G. A., & Steinfeldt, M. C. (2011). Drive for Muscularity and Conformity to Masculine Norms Among College Football Players. *Psychology Of Men & Masculinity, 12*(4), 324-338.

Turkle, S. (2012). *Alone Together*. NY: Basic Books.

White House Council on Women and Girls and the Office of the Vice President (2014). *Rape And Sexual Assault: A Renewed Call To Action*. Retrieved from http://whitehouse.gov

When the News Reports on Higher Education Accountability, What Does the Public Read and Hear?

Charles L. Carney

Abstract. On all levels of government in the U.S., ever-tightening budgets have meant ever-increasing calls for accountability for the agencies they fund. The term accountability has become a "cultural keyword" applied to publicly responsible agencies, fashionable and often favoured by politicians and policymakers with the intent to make sure agencies spend dollars wisely or at least give an appearance of such concern. Public higher education institutions have contended with growing accountability measures over the last four decades, a time when state dollar support for these institutions has consistently shrunk. It is a new economic dynamic for institutions that continues to develop both at the state and federal levels, most recently with President Obama's call for a ratings system for higher education institutions. Reflecting that dynamic, media coverage has focused upon many of the matters central to policymaker and politician concerns. Economic value, quantification of resources, affordability, and quality have dominated the extant analyses of media coverage concerning higher education accountability. Examining the most recent decade of available documents, this study examines coverage of higher education accountability by the *New York Times*, an internationally-influential publication shown to have significant agenda-setting influence on how other media outlets portray a news story. Utilizing a technique of ethnographic content analysis, the study discerns themes and keywords predominant in coverage surrounding higher education accountability. Higher education leaders should be cognizant of these themes to understand how they should respond; media outlets should examine the themes to determine whether coverage of higher education accountability is of significant depth.

Keywords: higher education media coverage, accountability

Introduction

It is common that trustees, lawmakers, and others across the United States ask pointedly whether a college degree is worth the investment and whether institutions are fulfilling the prime mission of higher education -- also a matter of debate. Whether colleges should ensure graduates have work skills for a job or develop critical thinking is often an element of such inquiries. Showing accountability for resources, contributions to the economy and society, and intellectual value is an everyday reality for postsecondary institutions. At the same time, diminishing state budget support has increased pressure for colleges and universities to find more resources to support the higher education mission.

Within this environment, media presentations about higher education often highlight these competing pressures. Typically, news presentations use a narrative focused primarily on affordability, quality, and accountability for results (Espinosa, 2014). Such coverage reflects what Alexander (2000) called a "new economic dynamic" (p. 427) view of higher education that has become "utilitarian," (Ibid., p. 427) focused on economic values and quantification of resources. To determine a pattern of such coverage over the last decade, this study examines news reports in *The New York Times* to discern themes and patterns of coverage that can provide insight into what information the public receives about higher education accountability.

Accountability and higher education

Accountability has become a "cultural keyword" used more frequently in public discourse over the last four decades (Dubnick, 2014). Dubnick defined accountability used as "institutionalization" (p. 28) as intended to convey constraining power and fostering responsiveness of officials to make them answerable. He also noted that accountability can be used in a discourse of "incentivization," (Ibid., p. 28) [1] providing standards and metrics designed to influence behaviour. Education accountability is in keeping with similar efforts to promote government return on investment, and encompasses both institutionalization and incentivization.

Accountability for higher education has been driven by quite a few commissioned reports dealing specifically with the performance of higher education institutions in the last decade, including "Measuring Up 2004: the National Report Card on Higher Education" and 2005's "Cracks in the Education Pipeline" with the subtitle "A Business Leaders Guide to Education Reform," published by the National Center for Public Policy and Higher Education. In 2006, U.S. Secretary of Education Margaret Spellings unveiled her plan for the Commission on the Future of Higher Education, popularly known as "The Spellings Commission," noting the shortcomings of higher

---

[1] Dubnick's term "incentivization" is accountability based on the premise that humans respond positively to information about their performance. It outwardly provides for the agency implementing accountability the "promise of performance." Accountability is used in "institutionalization" as a built-in mechanism with the "promise of democracy" (pp. 28-29).

education while laying out a design to provide federal funds to states that collect and publicly report how well students learn (Lederman, 2006). More recently, President Barack Obama instructed the U.S. Department of Education to develop a ratings system for higher education institutions that could tie federal funding to the employment of graduates and their salaries, in a vein similar to what the publication *Consumer Reports* produces for consumer goods (Stratford, 2013).

At the same time, surveys have shown a steady increase in public concern over the cost of college, yet ambivalence about particular action that the government should take to ease it (Immerwahr, 2004; Immerwahr & Johnson, 2007; National Center for Public Policy and Higher Education, 2008). This growing concern made the matter of higher education cost one of the most important issues in recent presidential elections (Selingo, 2008).

Media coverage of higher education

The power of the media to shape public opinion is contained in the manner in which it presents issues to the public (Entman, 2004). News stories typically emphasize certain points in a story more than others so that the overarching message of a news report leans more toward a certain segment of facts and opinions than others. This is the "frame" of the story, the very broad thematic emphasis of a news report and its central organizing theme (Altheide, 1996; Gamson & Modigliani, 1989).

News stories about higher education have typically been framed in a few specific ways. Ratcliff (1995) characterized reporters covering higher education as taking on certain role orientations including that of a "consumer advisor," "policing universities," as a "window to university," covering "politics of higher education," covering "higher education trends," and covering "social trends" (pp.11-12). A recent content analysis of higher education news coverage found three particular themes as the centrepiece: 36 percent characterized higher education as an economic engine for society, 19 percent focused on issues of access and affordability, while 15 percent emphasized matters of institutional budget problems (Wilson, 2009). As public concern on college cost has risen, emphasis on cost at high-priced institutions without context of student financial aid, discounts, or alternatives may be "fanning the flames of anxiety" for anxious higher education consumers" (Stanfield, 1998, p.135).

Methodology, Significance of *The New York Times*

The technique of ethnographic content analysis or ECA (Altheide, 1996; Altheide & Grimes, 2005; LeGreco & Tracy, 2009) was used to examine the news stories within the sample of study. The purpose of ECA is to understand the communication of meaning by developing emergent coding categories based on the examination of the text (Altheide, 1996, p.2). Using the Lexis-Nexis database, 144 articles containing both the keywords "higher education" and "accountability" were pulled from publication between the dates of Jan. 1, 2005 and Jan 1, 2015. An analysis of those documents pared the final selection of articles to 30. Articles were taken out of consideration if the reference to accountability was not germane to the point of the story. Articles with a primary focus on K-12 education, not higher education, were also excluded.

The New York Times (NYT) is the third-largest U.S. newspaper by circulation and is considered the national newspaper of record (Benoit, Stein, and Hansen, 2005). Placement of a story on the front page of the *NYT* makes a story newsworthy for other media (McCombs & Reynolds, 2009), making it the agenda-setter for other media outlets (Golan, 2006; Bartels, 1996.) It is, therefore, a good barometer of general themes of coverage on a variety of issues.

Results

The articles were coded with pre-selected categories, based on review of the studies cited above. The original codes were "access and affordability," "are students learning?," "budget problems," "higher education value," "poor leadership," "quality," "research," "teaching," and "trends in higher education." After conducting analysis of about half of the documents, emergent categories were added in keeping with ECA protocol. The emergent categories were "purpose of college," "completion," and "government intervention."

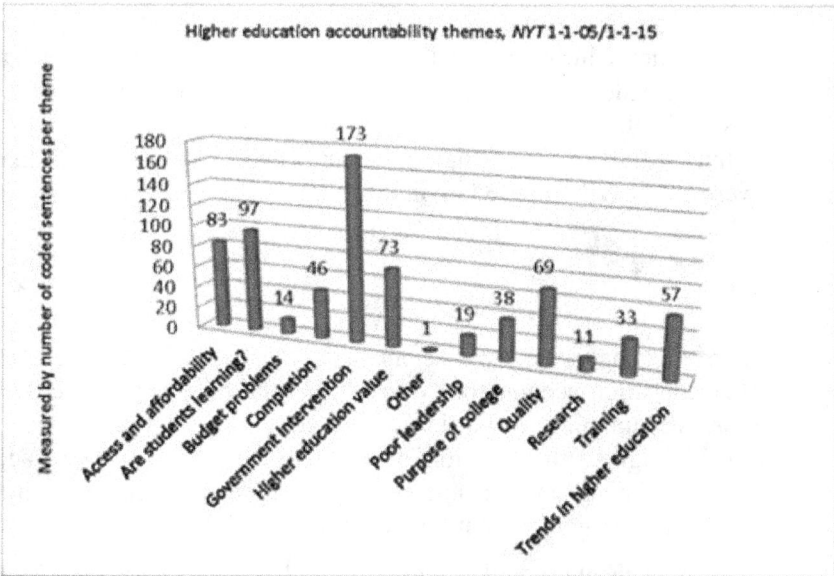

Fig. 1. Results from 714 coded sentences over 10 years of *New York Times* coverage of stories regarding higher education accountability

In all, there were 714 coded sentences throughout the selected articles (Fig.1). The emergent code of government intervention appeared the most often, with sentences coded for this 173 times, approximately 24 percent of all codes. This was true in stories especially from 2006 and 2007 in the wake of the Spellings Commission on Higher Education reports. An article from Feb. 9, 2006 had 25 such codes alone, with key sentences such as "What is clearly lacking is a nationwide system for comparative performance purposes using standard formats" (Arenson, 2006, Feb. 9, p.1A). Government intervention was a dominant frame, and upon a first reading of texts became a clearly preeminent theme for the stories.

All other codes were used more than 10 percent less than government intervention. "Are students learning?" (97 coded sentences) was a popular theme in many stories, coming in at 14 percent of all codes. It is a dominant sub-theme to government intervention, such as in that same Feb. 9, 2006 article, referencing government intervention and what it might do, looking to Texas as a model: "...they directed the university's nine campuses to use standardized tests to prove students were learning" (Arenson, 2006, Feb. 9, p. 1A).

Other codes over 10 percent included "access and affordability" (83 coded sentences, or 12 percent), "higher education value" (73 coded sentences or 10 percent)," and "quality" (69 coded sentences or 10 percent). Many articles highlighted "higher education trends" as a method of illustrating what is happening nationwide (8 percent) and "college completion" (6 percent) and the "purpose of college" (5 percent) got some attention. A possible telling finding is that "teaching" (less than 5 percent) and "research" (less than 2 percent) were not heavily focused upon in articles.

Conclusion

The results of this analysis are consistent with recent studies of news content about higher education accountability issues. While this analysis focused on stories about accountability in particular, the stories focused on government intervention highlighted the "economic driver" issues and matters of access and affordability. The discussion surrounding government intervention in this analysis has centred largely on matters of money.

It is telling that teaching and research, what higher education institutions would consider a prime directive, is not highly discussed in these contexts. The message to higher education institutions and supporters may well be that they must increase the visibility and demonstrate the value of their work. At the core of the accountability measures covered in these stories are matters measured by dollars. Higher education must be able to place such value on its mission to earn needed attention. While higher education institutions may not wish to concede to the new economic dynamic that this sort of coverage reflects, institutions and supporters must provide some semblance of return on investment to be clear about higher education value.

The analysis also makes clear that government intervention is driving the discussion; nearly a third of the articles came from the discussion surrounding the Spellings Commission in 2006. Further examples arose more recently when the Obama administration began promoting its ratings proposal for higher education institution. This suggests that higher education is constantly reactive, which makes controlling the discussion of what is valued more problematic. The public is hearing first from higher education critics; postsecondary leaders have to begin the discussion more often. Higher education leaders and institutions should take this as a cue to lead the discussion on accountability in order to shape it and also to be sure the discussion itself is focusing on the correct and proper matters for improving higher education overall.

References

Alexander, F. K. (2000). "The changing face of accountability: Monitoring and assessing institutional performance in higher education." *Journal of Higher Education*, 411-431.

Altheide, D. L. (1996). *Qualitative media analysis*. Thousand Oaks, CA:Sage Publications, Inc.

Altheide, D. L., & Grimes, J. N. (2005). "War programming: The propaganda project and the Iraq War." *The Sociological Quarterly*, 46(4), 617-643.

Arenson, K (2006, Feb. 9). "Panel Explores Standard Tests for College." *The New York Times,* p. 1A.

Bartels, L. M. (1996). Politicians and the press: Who leads, who follows? In *Annual Meeting of the American Political Science Association, San Francisco.*

Benoit, W. L., Stein, K. A., & Hansen, G. J. (2005). New York Times coverage of presidential campaigns. *Journalism & Mass Communication Quarterly*, 82(2), 356-376.

Dubnick, M. (2014). Accountability as Cultural Keyword in M. Bovens, RE Goodin & T. Schillemans (Eds.) *The Oxford Handbook of Public Accountability*, (pp. 23-38). Oxford: Oxford University Press.

Entman, R. M. (2004). *Projections of power: Framing news, public opinion, and US foreign policy.* Chicago, IL: University of Chicago Press.

Espinosa, L. C., Jennifer R., Tukibayeva, M. (2014). "Rankings, Institutional Behavior, and College and University Choice: Framing the National Dialogue on Obama's Ratings Plan." American Council on Education. Retrieved Jan. 15, 2015 from the World Wide Web: http://www.acenet.edu/news-room/Documents/Rankings-Institutional-Behavior-and-College-and-University-Choice.pdf .

Gamson, W. A., & Modigliani, A. (1989). "Media discourse and public opinion on nuclear power: A constructionist approach." *American Journal of Sociology*, (1)37.

Golan, G. (2006). "Inter-media agenda setting and global news coverage." *Journalism Studies*, 7(2), 323-333.

Immerwahr, J. (2004). Public attitudes on higher education: A trend analysis, 1993 to 2003. National Center Report Number 04-2. *Public Agenda*.

Immerwahr, J., & Johnson, J. (2007). Squeeze Play: How Parents and the Public Look at Higher Education Today. National Center Report 07-4, *Public Agenda*.

Lederman, D. (2006). "The Spellings Plan. Inside Higher Ed." Retrieved September 20, 2013, from the World Wide Web:

http://www.insidehighered.com/news/2006/09/26/spellings#sthash.uBKjCUDM.dpbs

LeGreco, M., & Tracy, S. J. (2009). "Discourse tracing as qualitative practice." *Qualitative Inquiry*, *15*(9), 1516-1543.

McCombs, M. E., & Reynolds, A. (2009). How the news shapes our civic agenda, in Bryant, J., and Oliver, M.B. (Eds.) *Media effects: Advances in theory and research*, 1-16. New York, NY: Routledge.

National Center for Public Policy and Higher Education. (2008). "Is college opportunity slipping away?" Retrieved February 20, 2015, from the World Wide Web: http://www.highereducation.org/pa_college_opp/

Ratcliff, G. R. (1995). The Press as a Policy Actor and Agent of Social Control and the Efforts of Universities to Negotiate Press Performance. The Association for the Study of Higher Education Annual Meeting Paper.

Stanfield, R. L. (1998). The media and public perceptions of tuition costs in Maeroff, G.I. (Ed.), *Imaging education: The media and schools in America*, 135–146. New York, NY: Teachers College Press.

Stratford, M. (2013). Obama Administration Seeks Input on How to Develop Ratings. Retrieved Jan. 23, 2014,, from http://www.insidehighered.com/quicktakes/2013/12/17/obama-administration-seeks-input-how-develop-ratings#ixzz2rHQBbzGm

Wilson, T. A. (2009). The role of communication messages and public relations strategies in the higher education public good debate: A study of four public research universities (doctoral dissertation). Retrieved from http://repositories.lib.utexas.edu/bitstream/handle/2152/6653/wilsont51105.pdf?sequence=2.

www.ingramcontent.com/pod-product-compliance
Lightning Source LLC
Chambersburg PA
CBHW050552280326
41933CB00011B/1815